Vital Nourishment

Translated by Arthur Goldhammer

Vital Nourishment

Departing from Happiness

François Jullien

ZONE BOOKS · NEW YORK

2007

The publisher would like to thank the French Ministry of
Culture — Centre National du Livre — for its assistance
with this translation.

Printed in the United States of America.

Distributed by The MIT Press,
Cambridge, Massachusetts, and London, England

First published in France as *Nourrir sa vie: À l'écart du
bonheur* © 2005 Éditions du Seuil.

Library of Congress Cataloging-in-Publication Data

Jullien, François, 1951–.
    [Nourrir sa vie. English]
    Vital nourishment : departing from happiness /
François Jullien ; translated by Arthur Goldhammer.
        p.   cm.
    Includes bibliographical references.
    ISBN 978-1-890951-80-1
    1. Life. 2. Meaning (Philosophy)
    3. Philosophy, Chinese. I. Title.

BD431.J7813 2007
128 — dc22   2007023996

Contents

Preface

This essay concludes a series of writings on the question of "living." To think through the concept of living from a detached position is far from easy. Unlike the notion of "life," it resists abstraction; its specific form does not emerge in the very act of contemplation. Living is a form of capital that must be nurtured and maintained; it concerns the hygiene of longevity. I have already explored this notion of "living" in two earlier works. In *Un sage est sans idée*, I examined variations on apothegms derived from philosophical constructions that pursued knowledge and truth.[1] And in *Du "temps,"* I explored the concepts of transition and duration, the phenomenology of the moment and of seasonal existence, as opposed to a notion of time delineated by "a beginning" and "an end," a product of European physics insofar as it hastens existence toward its End.[2] Those essays led to a schism between "living" and "existing." That schism in turn cried out to be supplemented by another divide, between *coherence*, arising out of the breakdown of barriers between opposites, and the logic of *sense* made dramatically taut by the question why (in *L'ombre au tableau*).[3] Finally, there was the subject of painting itself, the nonobjective object, transcending all others (the painter, in the Greek definition, is the *zoographos*, or, as the Chinese say, the "animation of the living" (see *La grande image n'a pas de forme*).[4]

Living has no meaning (except by way of projection or fabulation), nor is it absurd (despite the spiteful reaction of disbelief); it is *beyond meaning*. That is why approaching the question of living by way of vital potential or capital seems to me salutary: that way, the ineluctable distortions of ideology are kept to a minimum.

Where can one begin in thought if not with some opening, to be followed like a fissure to deposits more deeply hidden?

The crack I shall follow passes between Chinese and European thought. Each time I strike at a particular point with my pick, I open the fracture a little wider, until I expose certain notional lodes lying on one side or the other, deposits unrelated to one another but yielding riches in their respective domains. Having thus deepened the opposition, I look anew at the conditions under which European reason became possible, with an eye to unsettling the obvious and reconfiguring the range of the thinkable.

My starting point is a very common Chinese expression: "to feed one's life." It eludes the great divides between body and soul and between literal and figurative through which European culture has so powerfully shaped itself. Yet today we see what was consequently repressed returning to menace the contemporary mind, solicited as it is by the temptations of exoticism.

Pulling a bit on this thread of "vital nourishment," I see the mesh of our categorical oppositions begin to fall apart: not only at the level of the psychic and the somatic but also on the series of planes we distinguish as vital, moral, and spiritual. The goal is to recover some sort of wholeness of experience from the depths of the verb "to feed" when it is freed from these operational distortions — to the point where the idea of finality so commonly projected onto it is eliminated and the appeal to happiness, to which we aspire, dissolves. Indeed, might not the Chinese literati, in freeing themselves from the pressure of sense or meaning, be tell-ing us that the ability to "feed life" is simply the ability to maintain one's capacity to evolve by refining and decanting what is vital in oneself, so as to develop that vitality to the full?

What this journey affords is, once again, an opportunity to verify that the thought of the other remains inaccessible unless one is willing to rework one's own.

In this reworking, one's "own" thought ceases to exist. The purpose of dialogue between cultures is not to attach labels indicating what belongs to what, but rather to create new opportunities, to give philosophy a fresh start.

The Chinese text that I follow in this study is attributed to Zhuangzi (or Zhuang Zhou or Chuang-Tzu, circa 370–286 BCE), especially Chapters Three and Nineteen, "On the Principle of Vital Nourishment" and "Access to [Comprehension of] Life." What remains of this author's work is, of course, a corpus that was assembled six centuries later and is of a rather composite nature. Usually I name Zhuangzi himself as the author of the "inner chapters" of this work, which are the most authentic and certainly come from the hand of Zhuang Zhou; as for the later chapters of the work (the "outer" and "miscellaneous" chapters), I use the italicized form *Zhuangzi* in order to mark the different status of these texts when necessary.[5]

At the end of the book, I bring in a thinker from the period of the *Zhuangzi* compilation, Xi Kang, who wrote a celebrated essay inflecting the philosophy of vital nourishment in the direction of hygiene and longevity.

At times I use the general expression "Chinese thought." To avoid misunderstanding, let me say that I am not extrapolating some overall unity to a body of thought seen from a distance from the texts under examination. Nor do I regard it as somehow eternal, ignoring its extreme diversity or historical development. I am referring to Chinese thought as a product of *its language*, that is, a body of thought articulated in Chinese (just as Greek thought is that which speaks Greek).

CHAPTER ONE

Feeding the Body/Feeding the Soul:

The Symbolic Divide

"To feed" is the most basic verb, the most fundamental, the most rooted. It expresses the primordial activity, the primary, basic function, the act "I" engage in even before I am born or begin breathing. Because of it I belong to the earth, forever. Like the smallest animal crawling in the dirt, like the smallest plant, I began by feeding myself. It was through feeding that activity began in me, and it is that activity — which we cannot dream of shedding, which guides us with its rough hand, with the iron hand of hunger, where fate begins — that defines the most general class to which we belong: "we" living things. At the same time, the verb "to feed" lends itself to a variety of transpositions, insinuating itself — and leading us — into the most elaborate parts of the lexicon: I nurse a desire, a dream, or an ambition (in French: *je nourris*, from *nourrir*, to feed); reading feeds the mind; my mind feeds on fantasy; my style is undernourished; and so on. On the one hand, "to feed" is a verb that imposes its own meaning: blunt, raw, stark, and irrefutable, the factual in its unadulterated state, allowing no room for guesswork or ambiguity, no notion of variation or softening, no possibility even of imagining that the word lacks a perfect counterpart in every tongue. It is eternally the same and endlessly repeated, much as the very act of feeding indefatigably repeats itself in our lives: if

11

I do not feed myself, I die. On the other hand, "to feed" introduces the most distinctive and perhaps even ideal requirements. It reveals and promotes other levels and other resources, which emerge as vocations or even destinations: the divine is what helps to feed the winged apparatus of the soul, Plato tells us. For while the soul soars in pursuit of the gods, grazing in the pastures of truth, the contemplation of true realities is its "nourishing food." Or, the soul "feeds" on music, *en mousikē hē trophē*.

We know how the philosophy of language reined in this nascent disorder at its inception. Or, to put it another way, we know how easily this proliferating usage was brought back under control: it was enough to distinguish between the literal and the figurative senses. Just as I feed my body, said Plato, I feed my soul: the relationship is analogic. I posit two planes or segments, and at the same time I assume some "kinship" (*sungeneia*) between them. Thus the meaning of "feed" was bifurcated as the great codification opposing body and soul, or material and spiritual, required. It straddled the great divide between the visible and the invisible, the latter conceived as the intelligible. But such a classification is premature, is it not? And is it quite as self-evident as it seems? Does it not threaten to obscure the full experience of feeding? Or does it not, at any rate, threaten to obscure "experience" insofar as it remains complete, in the sense of being both fundamental and comprehensive, or "vital," that is, the experience of survival, development, and refinement? Because "feeding" also serves to express the ideal. As fundamental as it is, why should it not retain something of the unitary? In other words, why should it not establish within itself a relation other than one of analogy? Why must we plunge ourselves immediately into this alternative: to feed the body *or* (metaphorically) to feed the mind (feeling, spirit, aspiration)?

This split is fundamental. Hence we must begin by examining it anew so that the presuppositions of our thinking can be questioned. For nowadays everyone knows, or at least intuits, that this division marks an important fork in the road, the place where the fate of the so-called "Western" mind was historically decided. Indeed, Western religious tradition merely sanctioned a decision already inscribed in language: the true "hunger" is for the word of God; its mysteries are "food"; and the Lord has gathered for us the "bread" of Scripture. Christ gave us the bread of life. "Carnal" nourishment is rejected in favor of "heavenly" nourishment. And so on. Thus patristic discourse, comfortably adapting itself to this distinction between the material and the celestial, two worlds it was unembarrassed to treat always in parallel, speaks of the "milk" that feeds novices in the faith, the "vegetables" used to treat those still sick with doubt, and the more solid and substantial nourishment reserved for the elect in the form of "the flesh of the Lamb." Manna already symbolized this future nourishment, because, as Origen tells us, in order to have manna one must not "remain seated" but must "go out of the camp," that is, the body in which the soul is imprisoned.[1] Thus to react by seeking, as André Gide did, to return to the "fruits of the earth" (*les nourritures terrestres*), fails to escape the symmetrical alternative of concrete *or* symbolic in which we are trapped.[2] Although we have ceased to believe, and although we go on trying to secularize our thinking, we have not unlearned the implicit division to which our language hews so closely, for its convenience is undeniable.

In Chinese, however, we learn the common, everyday expression *yang sheng*,[a] "to feed one's life," and it unsettles the supposedly unshakable division described above. Its pertinence begins (discreetly, to be sure) to be less self-evident. For the meaning of "to feed one's life" cannot be narrowly concrete and material, but neither does it veer off into the spiritual, for the life in question here is not "eternal life." Though no longer reductively terrestrial, the meaning also resists tilting toward the celestial. "My

13

life," comprehended globally, is my vital potential. These were the terms in which the first "naturalist" thinkers in ancient China, reacting against any subordination of human conduct to any transcendent order whatsoever, be it religious or ritual, defined human nature: "Human nature is life," nothing more.[3] To feed one's life is the same as to feed one's nature. My entire vocation and sole responsibility lie in the care I take to maintain and develop the life potential invested in me, or — as another common expression puts it, elaborating on the same theme — in the care I take to nourish its essence or, rather, its "quintessence," its "flower," its "energy,"[b] by preserving its "cutting edge."[c] In other words, not only must we replenish our strength even as we expend it but we must also perfect our abilities by cleansing our physical existence of impurities, we must hone our edge while also maintaining "our form" (though the "form" in question refers to more than just the shape of our bodies). Another common expression, which might be translated literally as "feeding calm,"[d] can hardly be understood literally; to do so would yield too narrow an interpretation, made rigid by the projection of our grammar and thereby cutting off understanding. More loosely interpreted (and making good use of that looseness), the expression means to "nurture" and restore our strength by availing ourselves of peace and quiet, that is, to take our rest, to recover our serenity, to "re-create" ourselves, by withdrawing from the world's everyday cares and concerns. It is neither physical nor psychological — or, if one still wants to insist on these rubrics, it is both at once. This indissoluble unity is invaluable: it will, *provisionally*, guide our inquiry. To take another example, "to study life," *xue sheng*,[e] means in this context not to study what life is (as it would be if defined from the point of view of knowledge) or how to live (as it would be if defined from the point of view of morality) but to learn to deploy, preserve, and develop the capacity for life with which we are all endowed.[4]

Thus the ground shifts, undermining philosophy even before it *is* philosophy, by which I mean before philosophy conceives what it conceives (before it conceives *of* conceiving), prior to whatever choices and questions are within its power to make explicit. In his nomenclature of the living, Aristotle distinguishes and names three types of souls: the nutritive, the sensitive, and the thinking. The nutritive soul (*threptikē*), which subsumes animals and plants along with man, is primary; it is the basis of the other two. Yet at the beginning of the *Nicomachean Ethics*, Aristotle explicitly excludes life that feeds and grows but is also subject to corruption from his consideration of human life: "Life seems to be common even to plants, but we are seeking what is peculiar to man. Let us exclude, therefore, the life of nutrition and growth."[5] It is easy to see that the specificity of man's development will be sought in the realm of thought and knowledge, of *nous* and *logos*, at the (distinct) level of the "theoretical." To divert attention from the generic functions of nutrition and growth and thus to dissociate intellectual activity from organic life in an effort to conceive of man's "essence" and his development is, of course, fraught with consequences. Note, however, that ancient Chinese thought went in exactly the opposite direction: it deliberately turned away from the activity of knowing, which is endless and thus hemorrhagic in terms of energy and vitality, in order to concentrate on man's ability to use and preserve the vital potential vested in him. Take, for example, one of the most profound ancient Chinese thinkers, Zhuangzi, a contemporary of Aristotle's, whose thought I shall be exploring in this book. Consider the opening sentences of his chapter "On the Principle of Vital Nourishment": "Your life has a limit, but knowledge has none. If you use what is limited to pursue what has no limit, you will be in danger [of exhaustion]. If you understand this and still strive for knowledge, you will be in danger [of exhaustion] for certain."[6]

15

Both philosophers thus begin with renunciation, but the two renunciations are diametrically opposed. Where does renunciation take us, however, if it is no longer toward mind — the *nous* of the Greeks? Zhuangzi explains this in a crucial passage, which cannot be translated without a gloss, since it draws explicitly on Chinese medical art. If one no longer follows the endless and aimless path of knowledge, one must return to the source of our physical being, to a very different organ, namely the *principal artery* (du)[f], which traverses the back from the base of the spine to the base of the neck and conveys the subtle breath of life that allows this vessel to regulate our energy. The *influx* of energy passes through the empty interior of this artery, from its base to its summit, without deviating from its designated path. This is the "line" of life, the rule and norm of conduct to which we must cleave. This shift in focus is fundamentally important: it stops the dissipation of thought in knowledge and removes us to the vital median axis where organic regulation is maintained moment by moment. Only in this way, Zhuangzi concludes, can we "preserve our person," "complete our vitality," and "live out all our years to the end."

In order to appreciate the significance of this reorientation toward organic vitality and away from the temptation of knowledge (a temptation the Chinese clearly also felt), we must first recognize that the ancient Chinese had no conception of immortality. Since their world, unlike that of the Plato's *Phaedo*, had no *other-world* to which escape was possible, the only conceivable duration of existence was the embodied life of individual beings. Life as such did not persist in the souls that ascended to mingle with the winds of yang, nor in those that returned to the earth to merge with the energies of yin. Henri Maspero — though still unduly influenced, in my view, by European terminology — summed this up by saying that for Daoists, the "eternal life" of "salvation" meant "long life,"ᵍ understood "as a form of material immortality of the body itself."[7] The ground suddenly opens beneath our feet: can a body hope for such longevity when the process of achieving it must be seamlessly integrated with the phenomenal world?

Zhuangzi thus allows for a different type of dream, or, more notionally, for a different "ideal." If it is not of this world, at least it is *of this life*, insofar as this life must be "fed." Although he posits no paradise (not without evasiveness, at any rate), he is pleased to describe beings who — like the genies of distant Mount Gushi, who fed on wind and dew, and the Old Woman — have skin "as bright as snow" and retain "the delicacy and freshness of virgins," or "the complexion of infants." "After a thousand years," they tire of this world and ride the clouds back to the empyrean, following a "way," *dao*, which is precisely what wisdom claims to teach and which Zhuangzi characterizes by the verb *shou*:ʰ to know how "to keep" by purifying.[8]

The Old Woman, when asked about her childlike complexion, uses expressions that will at first seem enigmatic (to be patiently elucidated, avoiding all haste). By clarifying and decanting day after day (exactly what is being clarified is not discussed here, because only through gradual renunciation does "it" become perceptible), I come little by little to treat the "whole world," "things," and even "life" itself as "external" and therefore no longer a burden on my vitality. I then gain access to the "transparency of morning," thereby making visible a form of "independence" that is the only "absolute." There, "past and present abolish each other," and even in the midst of this "tumult" nothing stands in the way of "placidity."[9] Once attained, this placidity preserves longevity and "feeds" life. Elsewhere in this corpus, Zhuangzi writes that if the troubles of the outside world are shut out so that they are neither seen nor heard, the last screens disappear, leaving us face-to-face with "clear tranquillity," and "we no longer exhaust our physical being," no longer "rattle" or shake our "quintessence" (about this key term, which we have already encountered, I shall have more to say later on).[10] At that point we *hold on to* "all the vitality of our physical being" and enjoy "long life."

I will not interpret this gradual, methodical access to the "transparency of morning," in which one "sees [the] alone [independent, emancipated, unique]," as a mystical experience because all of this is the Old Woman's response to a specific question, which is entirely concerned with being-in-life: "You are well on in years, yet you have the complexion of a young child. How do you do it?" Questioned as to her dao, the Old Woman describes how she unburdens herself of every vestige of a cumbersome, energy-sapping "exterior" so as to focus exclusively on her *inner* or *vital capacity*. This capacity after gradually purifying itself, at last communicates directly ("transparently") with the pure (full) regime of natural "processivity," with the "taoic" ("unique"), which consequently remains continually present. This is the key point. Although the youthful glow in question may require loftiness and transcendence in order to attain it, it is not to be interpreted figuratively, for it pertains to the non-aging of the physical being. By methodically abandoning all my external and particular investments and concentrations that consume and dissipate vitality (including those pertinent to my own life), I become one with its common source. At that stage, the youthful Old Woman tells us, I will be completely unencumbered and therefore know how to "remain in contact" with vitality's perpetual renewal, so that I will stop growing old.

But how is it that we ordinarily allow our attention to flow outward instead of concentrating on what lies within — the *vital* equivalent of a Pascalian diversion? The following anecdote provides a counterexample: while strolling idly in a chestnut grove at Diaoling, Zhuangzi sees a "strange magpie" that swoops down and grazes him in passing. Zhuangzi is astonished that despite the size of its wings the bird cannot fly well, and that despite its gigantic eyes it does not see him. Clearly the bird found itself suddenly unable to use its natural capacities. But why? Zhuangzi hikes up his robe and hastens off in pursuit of the bird, crossbow in hand. At this point he sees a cicada that has just found a nice cool place and "forgotten itself." Nearby, a praying mantis hides behind a leaf and, just as "heedless of its safety" as its prey, prepares to catch the cicada. The magpie, of course, has been following the two insects, thinking only of when it might grab them both; it was the lure of this advantage that caused the bird to also "forget its true nature." But has not Zhuangzi, in chasing the bird, made the same mistake? This thought continues to trouble him for days.[11] In pursuing an external profit, or at any rate seeking to satisfy his curiosity, which drew his attention to the coarse outside world, he neglected not his conscience (or moral being or ideal aspiration or anything of that sort) but his "own person," his individual "ego," which becomes "authentic" when divested of all external distraction. He too endangers his vital being by forgetting to maintain it. Zhuangzi speaks of "forgetfulness," expenditure, and therefore danger but not of error, much less of sin: in this world without final judgment or the hope of resurrection, the imperative is not to "save one's soul" but to *safeguard* one's vitality.

Why have I chosen to delve into the *Zhuangzi* and trace the development of a philosophy of the "vital" and its "nourishment"? The reason is not just that I see here a significant and, indeed, in many respects exemplary fork in the road away from the implicit choices inherited from Greek philosophy and responsible for its rich harvest. This path, of course, gives us an opportunity to adopt an "external" point of view, itself highly elaborate and self-conscious, from which to reconsider the theoretical prejudice (that of *theorein*) that shaped our mind (where "our" here refers to the Western "we," which grew out of the search for truth and freedom). I confess, though, that I am more interested in the very conditions of my own particular thought and, to that end, in how (that is, by what strategy) I can gain some perspective within my own mind. For this, the externality of Chinese thought, its deconstructive effect, is useful to me. I prefer this course to taking theatrically an overt position and proposing a "thesis," an exercise in which philosophy all too often indulges to demonstrate its prowess. This time, something else is at stake as well. Or, rather, the question of "feeding one's life" raises a new issue, which I saw emerging earlier but which here takes on a new dimension and obliges me to commit myself more openly. For clearly the attention ancient Chinese thinkers paid to feeding life, which is undoubtedly still among the most significant, influential, and durable traits of contemporary Chinese mores, ressonates with a major and growing concern among Westerners today, a concern that is in a sense *converting* many of them. In a dechristianizing world that no longer defers happiness to the hereafter, and which is by the same token less and less inclined to sacrifice in the name of a higher cause (be it revolution, fatherland, or what have you), we are in fact left, once we have rid ourselves of all these projections and associated hopes, with nothing other than the need to manage and maintain "that" which, if nothing else, at least cannot be suspected of being an illusion: namely, the *life capital* that is imparted to each individual being and that, stripped of all ideological guises, is said to be the only indubitable and therefore authentic "self."

As proof of this, I cite the extensive (sub)literature (on wellbeing, health, vitality, and so on) that flourishes today in magazines, on the fringes of the medical as well as the psychological without drawing much substance from either. This literature often makes reference to China, as if China were some sort of safety valve capable of liberating us from the powerful dualisms the West is now condemned to bear as its cross (and as if the great Western philosophers, including Plato and Descartes, had not themselves labored to transcend these same binaries). Today the philosophy sections of bookstores have been replaced with shelves devoted to an amorphous subject located somewhere between "Health" and "Spirituality." They are filled with books on "breathing," "energetic harmony," the "Dao of sex," ginseng, and soy. It hardly needs saying that this bastardized philosophy vaguely linked to the "East" and proliferating under cover of cloudy mysticism is terrifying. There is, of course, a big difference between the "undividedness" that will guide our inquiry — and whose theoretical consequences I wish to explore — and the troubled waters in which "self-help" propagandists fish for the easy profits to be reaped at the expense of indolent minds. My method is opposed to this, and that is why I cannot refrain from denouncing the guilty ideological conscience that has insidiously taken hold today. It is high time that ideas about breathing, harmony, and feeding be rescued from this pseudophilosophy and coherently integrated into the realm of philosophical reflection. Otherwise, Western thought may casually abandon the ideals it has constructed and plunge into a socially disastrous irrationalism. This essay is also, secretly and without any need to develop the point explicitly, political as well as philosophical.

Zhuangzi at least did not hide the thought which opposed the attention he devoted to feeding life: the debates between the philosophical schools, for example, which pitted the Mohists against the Confucians, and, more broadly, all the effort poured into argumentation, a practice which wastes energy (embodied for him by the sophist Hui Shi, whom he describes as sitting "with his back against an eleococca tree," consuming himself with dialectical refutations of the "hard" and the "white").[12] Also opposed

21

were heroism and the will to act: the "authentic men of the past" "did not train for feats of arms" or "make vast plans."[13] Ancient China was, of course, a culture without an epic. Zhuangzi also asked if one must sacrifice for the good of the world, gaining renown by giving up one's life so that "others might live."[14] Thus the question of feeding one's life also raised the question of what I believe is the most radical of human choices — more radical, in any case, than that between good and evil or *Hercules between Vice and Virtue* in our antique staging. Prior to the problem of values, which are always to one degree or another external, is the issue of the care and management of the self, the principle of which, we now know, is principally *economic*.

At this stage, we at last find *that which Zhuangzi did not envisage.* For while he had no difficulty seeing beyond morality (because concern for the good of course hinders the expression of vitality), he did not imagine how loss and pleasure (pleasure through loss) might be justified. Nor did he see what might justify a desire that, rather than consuming us because we failed to protect ourselves against it, is deliberately chosen and cultivated at the expense of longevity (even though all hope of immortality has been abandoned). Moreover, it is difficult to imagine how these two attitudes can be reconciled. Two possible attitudes exist toward the vital capital that is amassed through the "feeding" of the "self." Either we *preserve* it as best we can, purifying and decanting it so that it is not atrophied by the consuming pressure of the "exterior," by preoccupation, fear, or desire. Or, we act like Balzac's young hero Raphael, who negates in one orgasmic outburst all the meticulous effort devoted to preserving it, rushing "drunk with love" to his death in the lavish luxury of a Paris hotel. In this "last moment" he transforms the final spasm into apotheosis through the vigor of his violation: "no longer able to utter a sound, he set his teeth in Pauline's breast."[15]

CHAPTER TWO

Preserving the Freedom to Change

A break like Raphael's would be expenditure and its tragic challenge, confronting its limit. Or, in contrast, it could be the deliberate protection of one's potential, where, through an encounter with the philosophy of immanence, it develops into the *dao* of wisdom. For in addition to writing *about* one's desire, one can also write at a *distance* from it. Yet can this Chinese feeding of life become as intimate for us as Raphael's fate? We have stumbled upon a moment of resistance and it is precisely what we must take as our point of entry into this other form of intelligibility. My bias as a philosopher leads me to believe that what is commonly called "personal development" does not require us to convert but rather develops its own criteria for coherence. How can what we have designated both the *preservation* and the *purification* of something called the "self" come together in an articulated form? Or, to put it another way, how, by emancipating, decanting, and refining my physical being, do I learn to "preserve" its ability to grow and to develop my vitality to its full ("daoic") potential? Let us begin, we read at the beginning of one of the "outer" chapters of the *Zhuang-zi*, by eliminating all activities and all forms of knowledge extraneous to the desired telos: he "who has mastered the true nature of life" is not concerned with anything removed from life; he "who has mastered the true nature of fate" is not concerned with anything that does not influence that fate.[1] A series of conclusions follows. "To feed the body" one must "begin with material resources and goods." Yet even if "we have more than enough material resources and goods," "the body may still go unnourished." At a higher level, "in order to ensure our vitality," we must "begin by making sure that life does not leave our body." But we also know that "even if life does not leave our body ... our vitality may very well diminish." In other words, *Zhuangzi* concludes, contrary to what is all too frequently believed, "feeding the body is not enough to maintain vitality." Feeding the body is a necessary condition of vitality, but it is not sufficient. This leads logically to the central question: in addition to feeding the body, what else is necessary but not separable from it (thus ruling out something spiritual, as opposed to the physical), if I am to "feed" not only what I reductively call my body but also, and more essentially, or "quintessentially," my life?

Viewed solely in intellectual terms, the problem might be posed as follows: only by imagining what transcends my bodily form without divorcing itself from the physical, so that it vitalizes or energizes it, can I think of "feeding" in a unified way, avoiding the distinction between the literal and the figurative. But what mediation can effectively link these two distinct levels and thus banish *from my experience* the great dualism of the physical and the spiritual? On what grounds, that is, can I conceptualize this *qualitative elevation*, which does not *cut itself off* from the concrete (and therefore does not produce the famous "qualitative leap")? This mediation can be found in the transitional phase Chinese philosophy terms *the subtle*, or that which, without necessarily leaving the realm of the physical and concrete (and therefore without reference to the order of faith), is nevertheless already liberated from the encumbrances, limits, and opacities of the concrete.

24

Although the Chinese did not investigate different and distinct levels of "being," as the Greeks did in their search for pure knowledge, they were nevertheless passionately interested in the *refined* and *decanted*, which they believed was more "alive" because it was more fluid and less reified, and from which they hoped to derive the maximum effect.

There are various angles from which the subtle becomes accessible to experience. In aesthetics, for example, there is the exquisite flavor of the barely perceptible, whether in sound or image, in the transitional stage between silence and sonority in music or between emptiness and fullness in painting, when the sonic or pictorial realization is barely evident or on the verge of vanishing. Whether just barely outlined or already beginning to fade, the subtle ceases to impose the brute opacity of its presence and can no longer be confined. Diffuse, vivid, and insinuating, it continues to emanate indefinitely. In military strategy, the subtle refers to the flexibility and suppleness of a maneuver undertaken before forces are deployed on the ground, thereby rendering the opposition relatively inert. If I remain alert, I elude my enemy's grasp and my extreme responsiveness constantly replenishes my potential. Conversely, my adversary is hampered by the rigidity of his plans and deployments. I maintain myself in the agile posture of the virtual, while the other remains mired in or confined by the actual and thus vulnerable.

All Chinese practices derive from this. At precisely this point, *Zhuangzi* introduces a term mentioned earlier which points in this direction: the term we have begun to translate as "essence" or "quintessence," which might also be rendered as "flower," "choice," "elite," or "energy" (*jing*).[a] This belongs to the realm of the physical, but it is not raw; it has been refined. Originally it denoted the seed of selected or hulled rice, the *fine fleur* as one says of the germ of wheat in French, but it was also applied to human sperm,

25

to the spirit of wine, and indeed to any form of matter that has been decanted, subtilized, and thus energized and endowed with the ability to communicate its effect. For this reason it opposes the phase of the tangible, the opaque, the inert, the numb, and the crude. By using words such as "subtle," "spirit," and "quintessentialized," I am well aware that I may seem to be reintroducing an obscurantist vocabulary that predates the great conquests of Western science and its experimental, mathematical, and model-oriented rationalism, whose prodigious truth effects cannot be denied. Nevertheless, rather than avoid the word as a vestige of an archaic mentality, I have chosen to dwell on it: for besides the importance of this term in the *Zhuangzi*, it also provides us with an opportunity to use the parallel between Chinese thought and the history of our rationality to recover and rethink precisely those aspects of our most fundamental experience — the experience of life that modern Western science has covered up and obscured with its characteristic procedures (traditionally we have allowed this sort of thing a place only in alchemy, but only to exclude it all the more thoroughly). Nowadays we approach such matters only obliquely, by way of culturally repressed antirationalist, esoteric, and mystical categories, whose ill effects I deplored earlier. Our realm of intelligibility instead needs to welcome the "subtle" and "quintessential," which are the products of refinement and decantation and which bridge the gap between the concrete and the spiritual, the literal and the figurative. Zhuangzi has something to contribute to this task.

This will help us to grasp, in a form other than a moral *topos*, how the lack of concern with, and disengagement from, the affairs of the world recommended by both Eastern and Western wisdom can in fact *reinforce the vitality of the self*. *Zhuangzi* goes on to explain how, by committing myself ever more deeply to the process of emancipation, refinement, and decantation (compare the verbal repetition in Chinese, *jing er you jing*),[b] I simultaneously free myself from the fixations, stumbling blocks, and encumbrances — the crude screens that worldly affairs place in front of my inner flux and dynamism. I thereby restore the limpidity, subtlety, and alacrity of that flux and thus relate it ever more closely to the constant *influx* that links life to its source, both in myself and in the all-encompassing world process. For as the nutritional metabolism of my physical being already reveals at the most elementary level, and as the alternation of "concentration" and "dispersion" that marks the time of life and death exhibits on the cosmic scale, "feeding one's life," by entering into an ever-increasing subtilization (quintessentialization), will nonetheless always come down to this: "to remain open to change."[c] This is the first major point: nutrition is not progress toward something; it is renewal. The transformation that it brings about has no other purpose than to reactivate something (forsaking the problematic of sense to which the West is so attached: because life in itself makes no sense, as we know). Or, as Zhuangzi says earlier on the same page, in a formulation too concise to be translated literally: when I achieve "equality-placidity" by freeing myself from the "bonds" and impediments of worldly affairs and cares, I discover in myself the capacity for the natural transformation that perpetually irrigates the world. By connecting with this process and remaining in phase with its immanence (*yu bi*),[d] I put myself in a position to "modify-incite" and therefore to reconnect continually with life (in myself), rather than allow it to cling and adhere — to some investment, some representation, or some affect, as caring about things inclines us to do — and subsequently to stagnate and wither.

Here, though, there are grounds for disappointment. We had hoped to gain intimacy with the form of coherence associated with "nourishment," to the point where it became a life choice. Probing beneath the intricacies of our thoughts, we claimed to discover what was least abstract in them, the source of our vitality. But once this "nourishment" is no longer limited to the feeding of the "body," must it fly off into the realm of the speculative? How can we express that which constitutes experience without immediately splitting it in two? How can we construct it without losing it? A little later in the same chapter discussed earlier, we read about a prince, who asks a visitor a question: "I've heard that your master taught [how to nourish] life. What did you learn from this?" The guest offers an enigmatic answer: "I swept at the master's gate with a broom. What do you think I learned?" One might conclude that the guest is either avoiding the question or being modest, but I do not think that either is correct, because not to answer is in fact to provide an answer of sorts. It suggests that the questioner must make further progress before he can hope to be enlightened. More than that, however, the act of sweeping in front of the master's gate indicates in a most basic way that the visitor plays a discreet but effective role in the preservation and renewal of life. Frequently, particularly in Japanese temples, those who participate in the life of the temple sweep its stairs or wipe its banisters with a damp cloth, moving in a way that is neither nonchalant nor overexcited, neither hurried nor fatigued, cleaving to the form of things without pressing on them or breaking away from them. I believe that what we have here is an answer in the form of an action, or, rather, a movement, if I may put it that way: the movement of sweeping, which is repeated for each step. The prince fails to take in this answer, however, and is no doubt waiting for some theoretical content. His order elicits a laconic response: "I have heard my master say that to be good at nourishing life is like feeding sheep: if you notice some of the sheep straggling behind, you whip them."

An image comes readily to mind: sheep graze here and there,

and a few slowly wander away from the rest of the flock. Scattered across the countryside, they lag behind and slow the others' advance. But why sheep? Perhaps simply because the Chinese character *yang*, which signifies "to feed," is composed of the key for "food" and the root for "sheep." More surely, however, because the attitude one should take toward one's nourishment is the same as that adopted by the shepherd who allows his flock to proceed at its own pace, following its noses, while he keeps an eye out for stragglers. This shepherd does not lead the animals in his charge by marching at their head like the good pastor in the Gospels, who guides his flock across the desert to a lush and fertile promised land. I see the shepherd in the Chinese text as a master who is content to follow along behind his sheep, making sure that no dissident motivation leads them astray and that the flock as a whole continues to move forward. Progress lies not in moving toward a visible ideal but "merely," as I put it earlier, in remaining open to change.

The question thus remains as broad as possible. It cannot be reduced to moralizing introspection (the famous "examination of our conscience" one learns as a child). Its sole concern is efficacy: to move forward, but with an openness to the interior dimension. This can be understood equally well in physiological terms or in moral or psychological ones (what *lags behind in me*), and it can be interpreted as disposition, function, impetus, or feeling: what will I have to "whip" in order to restore order — the common order of my vital evolution — and to keep moving forward? It can be interpreted in a medical or pathological register as the way cells or organs seek to develop on their own, isolated from the function of the whole organism, so that they no longer evolve with the rest and either atrophy or turn cancerous. Or one can read it in a psychoanalytic mode: the neurotic remains attached to some event in his past, so that his psychic life ceases to evolve. Or he may

29

become "trapped" by some emotion in the wake of a pathogenic situation from which there is no exit. Or, in the most general sense, inertia is characteristic of the way the libido is invested, for psychoanalysis teaches us that it is always reluctant to abandon an old position for a new one and therefore tends toward paralysis through adherence and fixation.

The Chinese interpretation, proceeding as usual, insists that the "way" of *remaining open to change* requires valuing the median and therefore opposing any deviation toward either extreme. The prince's visitor eventually explains his meaning. Shan Bao lived among the cliffs and drank only water. He did not seek profit and was therefore not concerned with other men. He was thereby able to preserve his vital potential and reach the age of seventy without losing his childlike complexion. Unfortunately, he crossed the path of a hungry tiger, who, given the solitude in which Shan Bao lived, easily devoured him. Then there was Zhang Yi: he assiduously visited every single noble mansion and at the age of forty he was already weak inside and caught a fever, from which he died. "One fed his inside, but the tiger ate his outside, while the other fed his outside, but illness attacked him from within. Neither man applied the whip to what lagged behind." The path of true nourishment falls between the two. Make no mistake, however: the precise middle way is not equidistant from withdrawal, on the one hand, and social life, on the other, for such a middle path would also lead inevitably to immobility and impede life's renewal. The art of renewal instead lies in the alternation between tendencies. Confucius (whom Zhuangzi often portrays ironically but who is here acknowledged as an expert on the just middle) offers this comment: withdrawal "to the point of hiding" and cutting off relations with others (which leaves us alone and helpless when an external danger arises) is a mistake; so is activity so external that we are constantly exposed (to pressure, intrigue, and so on), deprived of relaxation, and eventually devoured by our preoccupations. The wrong lies not in one position or the other but in the attachment to a position, whatever it happens to be, to the point of becoming immobilized by it. We should not isolate ourselves in a certain position, lest we cut ourselves off from the opposite position and become deaf to calls to free ourselves from the position we happen to be in (so as to continue to advance); the alternative to this is necessity. Stuck in an extreme, life ceases to "feed" itself because it loses its virtuality, bogs down, becomes stalemated, and no longer initiates anything new.

In a laconic passage at the beginning of his chapter on feeding life, Zhuangzi makes the following point: "If you do good, do not seek renown. If you do evil, avoid punishment."[2] Ultimately it matters little whether the action is "good" or "evil": the important thing is not to become so attached to a position as to remain trapped by it. Even the good becomes a trap for vitality, not only when it becomes routine but also when we become prisoners of the label. This, moreover, is what we find embodied immediately thereafter in the *principal artery*, or *du*, which irrigates the back from bottom to top and is the vessel through which energy flows. Why does our attention, once liberated from the endlessly spendthrift thirst for knowledge, focus instead on this artery as defining the line and rule of life? Because, as we have already discussed, this median artery has a regulative capacity that ensures respiratory constancy. And what is respiration but a continual incitation not to dwell in either of two opposite positions — inhalation or exhalation? Respiration instead allows each to call upon the other in order to renew itself through it, thus establishing the great rhythm of the world's evolution, never absent from the Chinese mind: the alternation of day and night and the succession of the seasons. Thus respiration is not only the symbol, the image or figure, but also the *vector* of vital nourishment.

31

CHAPTER THREE

To Feed One's Life/To Force One's Life; Or, How the Attachment to Life Turns against Life

If we therefore isolate our "nature" from everything that encumbers, conceals, or hobbles it; if we liberate ourselves from ideological perspectives and constructs, then we can restore our nature to what it truly and uniquely is: the vital potential that we are. Since we do not believe in another life, we preserve this life, here and now. Defying imposed values, we "preserve" life from illusory sacrifices and vain desires of glory and success. But what does "preserve" mean when the object of preservation is life? Does it mean to guard life as we would guard a treasure (our only treasure, since it is the one value that remains intact when the whole fragile edifice collapses in rubble)? Is it to cling to life, to retreat into it by making it our chief concern? Is it to care for life by protecting it against all forms of aggression and dissipation? It is at this point that vital nourishment attains philosophical depth, setting itself apart from all the recipes for vitality and taking on a dimension that is not strictly moral but more radical still. For to preserve our life is not to focus exclusively on it; nor is it to contrive to bottle up the life that is in us in order to save it for as long as possible from its despised opposite, death. To preserve our life is to plumb the depths of our life in search of the vital logic of which loss is as legitimate a part as inception, expiration as inspiration, and thus to "keep" our life open to renewal through the alternation of the global life process. "To feed one's life" does not mean to strive to enhance or prolong it, to seek to force life to sustain itself and endure. Indeed, it is only through de-willing, de-possession, that life can sustain itself and endure. This is the sense, bordering on a paradox, that must be carefully cultivated so as not to confuse it with other banal conceptions. Hence close reading is essential.

Let us therefore retrace our steps. In the progressive ascent that allows the Old Man to "preserve" his youth and achieve "long life," we came across a statement that may seem surprising. The Old Man says that we must treat as "external," and hence of no importance for our vitality, not only "the world" and "things" but also "life."[1] Without dwelling on this passage so as to preserve the tension inherent in the formula, I interpret this as meaning that only if I liberate myself from [my concern with my] life will I achieve the "transparency of morning" and rise to the full potential of my vitality, without further depletion or weakening. Similarly, when we were asked to deliver ourselves from worldly affairs, whose power to retain and fixate impedes our dynamism and internal renewal, we were subsequently told, as if it were self-evident, that "if we free ourselves from the cares of the world, our physical being will no longer be depleted," but, stranger still, that "if we abandon life, the quintessence of our vital being (*jing*) will no longer be lacking."[2] Here, modern commentators vie to diminish what they take to be the bizarre meaning of this passage: "life," it is claimed, should be understood in a weak sense as "futilities" and "petty matters." This reading restores the expected conventional meaning: no one takes offense at the idea that it is enough to "give up" life's pettiness and trifles (the better to concern ourselves with life itself). If, however, we follow the traditional commentators, we are confronted with a jarring literal meaning: the recommendation is *to give up life itself*, including our preoccupation with our longevity, so that the "quintessence" of our vitality will no longer be in short supply but will instead replenish itself.

One passage in the Old Man's statement is even more incisive, on account of an antithesis: "That which kills life does not die; that which engenders life is not born," or so the translation usually runs, thus construing the subject of both halves of the antithesis — supposedly the *dao*, the subject *par excellence* — as sovereign over the life and death of all living things.[3] By virtue of this operation, the *dao* becomes God (and the passage in question becomes mystical). But a whole tradition of commentary interprets this passage quite differently. Recall that in Chinese, *sheng* means both "to live" and "to engender":[a] "That which rids itself of life does not die; that which seeks to live [or, better, lives to live, *sheng sheng*] does not live."[4] Or, as the gloss would have it, he who worries about preserving and prolonging life, and who "is therefore preoccupied" with his own life, who "values" and "clings" to it, "does not live." He who thinks only of his own life does not live, not so much because this tiresome concern with his own life interferes with his joy of living but, more radically, because it obstructs and corrupts the very source of his vitality. By contrast, according to the commentator Guo Xiang, he who achieves the "transparency of morning" after treating life itself as "external" no longer fears life and death but finds peace and tranquillity in whatever happens to him. His vitality "unfolds" on its own and avoids becoming "bogged down" in any form of attachment, including the attachment to life. He is then free to respond to the only stimuli that come his way, and thus he "lives" in the cool "transparency of morning."[5] Let us therefore preserve this strong reading by retaining only the perspective of vitality (the Old Man still has a child's complexion) and refusing to theologize it as we do when we hypostasize the subject. Otherwise, the sense of the expression is immediately assimilated by our Western tradition: God, the absolute power who is neither born nor dies, can both kill and engender life. Such are God's primary attributes, which theology aims to define. Instead, if we follow the Chinese interpretation, we raise ourselves to the absolute level of the great process, or *dao*; we "abandon" our own lives, we "eliminate" ("kill") all concern for our own lives, and then we no longer die. We no longer instigate in ourselves anything that can hobble our lives, whereas he who wants to live, "to live to live," is no longer alive. In order to live life fully (completely), we must not cling to life. If we do not take this route, we would not be able to understand two statements: one at the beginning of the chapter which states that "the height of knowledge" is to live out the natural course of our days and not to die prematurely, and the other, a little farther on, which says that the "authentic" man does not know "love life" or "detest death," for "neither does he rejoice at his coming" into the world "nor refuse to return" to the undifferentiated: "easy does he come" and "easy does he go."[6] There is nothing that he is not prepared to "welcome" when it comes. Likewise, there is nothing that he is not disposed to "see off" when it goes. The "authentic" man accepts this coming and going and is life's gracious guest or host in each circumstance.

He who "lives to live" does not live. As always, the text should be read as literally as possible and without fear of its radical implications: that he who clings to life and is always thinking about how "to live more" depletes the source of life within himself. Or that he who is horrified by the idea of death, his own death, and seeks to ward against it thereby closes his life off to the natural respiration through which life constantly replenishes itself in him. He who strives after life depletes his life proportionately. He focuses on his life and makes it his supreme and indeed his only value, for all other values are reduced to naught by comparison the moment he learns that his life is threatened and that the dizzying abyss has opened beneath his feet. At bottom, he cares about nothing else: he wants to live, he lives to live, to live more, to live at any price. But by clinging to life he loses the ability to embrace life in all its variability; he forgets how to allow life to come and go within him, as the sea ebbs and flows without and as he inhales and exhales the vital breath within. He loses the knack of "welcoming" the influx of life and "seeing off" the efflux in a single, unified, never-ending gesture of solicitation and compensation. He thus freezes the life within him, paralyzes it, and by his own action hastens its end. Clearly Zhuangzi would have had little use for the self-help formulas that unwittingly reveal a fear of aging and death and try desperately to ward them off. Too much concern with life and anxiety at the idea of losing it ultimately turns against it.

Chinese thought teaches us at every turn that one will never attain the exact center by "holding" or clinging to the Middle (the supreme value of the Confucians) because to cling is to freeze and immobilize and thus to miss the always-moving point of equilibrium, of regulation.[7] Nor is it by clinging to the Void (the supreme value of the Daoists) that we achieve emptiness, for then we reify it as if it were fullness, its opposite, and thus lose the perpetually animating effect of vacuity.[8] Similarly, it is not by grasping at life or becoming obsessed with it that we learn to "feed" it. If Zhuangzi elevates the idea of the vital to an absolute, and indeed because he does so, he cannot treat it as an object of targeted intentionality and possessive will. Life, like God, fundamentally permeates and transcends us. We cannot possess God exclusively but can only wish that his grace be bestowed upon us. The same goes for life, which we cannot possess for ourselves alone.

The other great ancient Daoist text, the *Laozi*, sets this forth as a principle: "The reason why Heaven and Earth are able to endure is that they do not live for themselves. This is how they become capable of longevity."[9] "To live by oneself"[b] or "for oneself" is the Laozi's way of saying that one is preoccupied with one's own life and thinks only of it. Heaven and earth, which give generously of themselves to feed others, do not seek longevity for themselves, and that is why they "endure." Living is not an aim in the sense that I want to live, to "live to live," evermore, at any price; it is, rather, a result, just as elsewhere in the Laozi we learn that it is not "by showing off" that we "gain renown" or "by imposing ourselves" that we "become illustrious."[10] Regardless of whether the desired result is longevity, glory, or success, it must come about on its own. It must follow from the initial conditions, including both the process upon which we embark and the resources we invest, rather than be sought after as such. Any effort we make to bring about the result is wasteful and stands in the way of the advent sponte sua of the desired outcome. He who seeks to force the result expends his potential. This maxim can be read quite broadly: in the end, it is only to the extent that "we do not seek to be great" that we can "achieve greatness."[11] Conversely, when we see people who exhaust their energy, we know that they have attached "too much importance" to "living to live" (sheng sheng): they squander their strength when they should "husband" it so as to preserve the vital potential they contain within them.[12] It is bad to "enhance" or "force" life (yi sheng),[c] because our "spirit" then uses up our energy to enhance our strength, so that we embark upon the cycle in which increase is the prelude to enfeeblement and apogee is the prelude to decline, and life ends in "premature death."[13]

What we have here, then, is a maxim stated as an absolute principle of existence that is disturbingly similar to a well-known passage of the Gospel. It is so similar that one wonders if some anthropological truth is being expressed, a truth couched, in the one case, in terms of the vital and, in the other, in terms of a division of the world into two realms: the here below which intersects with longevity, and the hereafter which corresponds to life everlasting. In any event, the antithetical power is the same, as is the way the attachment to life turns against life. "The man who loves his life will lose it, while the man who hates his life in this world will keep it for eternal life."[14] Here, "life," which translates the Greek *psuche*, or "soul," but corresponds to the Hebrew *nefesh*, refers in the Greek of the Septuagint and the New Testament both to man the living individual and to that which constitutes his "self," just as in the Daoist text. What is this thing that has but one meaning, that must ultimately be construed in just one way, whether it be in Greek, Hebrew, or Chinese? What is this thing — at once transreligious, transcultural, translinguistic, and trans-historical (because it makes its appearance beyond, or rather prior to, the various articulations that different languages deploy) — that might ultimately allow us to dispense with any "point of view" and grasp that which constitutes the common core, the essence of life? It is this: what is "specific" to life is precisely its ability to elude its own grasp. This cannot be stated as a precept except in a contradictory mode: he who loves life will lose it; and one must renounce life if one wants to live it. Thus is it written in the gospel of John: "Unless a kernel of wheat falls to the ground and dies, it remains only a single seed. But if it dies, it produces many seeds."[15] This passage might express the irreducible aspect of life that is compatible with life in all its forms, taking in and setting side by side the merely nutritive life of the vegetal and the fate of man. Thus, looking again at Zhuangzi and translating still more literally, we have "He who kills life does not die; he who lives to live does not live."

Now it becomes apparent where the difference arises that turns each of these thoughts irrevocably toward its distinctive destiny. In other words, we can see how a perception so radical that it is common to both the East and the West forks into two distinct conceptions, each of which now develops its own peculiar patterns and issues. In the Gospel of John, the kernel of wheat jumps from the realm of the concrete into that of the figurative. To reiterate the overarching parallel described earlier: the seed symbolizes Christ, the bread of life, whose Passion, prefigured in the passage quoted above, will guarantee the salvation of mankind. The food envisioned here, then, is food for the spirit. In the Daoist text, by contrast, there is no such gap between two different levels of meaning, and the logic of renunciation of life (or clinging to life) remains entirely within the realm of the vital. This produces a common logic of "effectiveness," whose fruits become apparent in a number of areas. Furthermore, it also yields a strategy. Laozi, by allowing the paradox free play, develops his most influential idea: in order to win at war, one must not strive for absolute strength but rather join "weakness" to strength, because the good general is not "martial" and water dominates the world by its "baseness."[16] In morality, great virtue "is not virtuous." It does not pursue virtue directly (nominally) but rather allows it to flow; lesser virtue, which "does not quit virtue," which attaches itself nominally and minutely to virtue, "is not virtuous," because it fails from the beginning to adopt the generous attitude of virtue, choosing instead to be meticulous and punctilious.[17] In aesthetics (though bear in mind that these distinctions of subject matter are derived from our Western tradition), a great work "avoids coming into the world entirely" and fulfills its goals all the more by renouncing the ambition to fulfill them.[18] This is why sketches are so valued — in a sketch, a work abandons itself so as to remain a work in progress rather than show itself off ostentatiously. And just as the best way to achieve an effect is to renounce all ambition to impose or prescribe one, so that instead of forcing the effect, one clears the way as much as possible for its emergence, so, too, do we clear the way for life to come by renouncing our attachment to it and refraining from any attempt to "enhance" or "force" it.

But what does it mean, exactly, to "enhance" or "force" life? As Zhuangzi defines it in a conversation with the sophist Hui Shi, to "enhance" and "force" life is to add a supplement to what life is in its natural course by giving in to the subjective temptation (qing)[d] "of the for and against" or "approbation-aversion."[19] One "forces" life by defending one argument and refuting another, as in the case where one conceptualizes the coexistence of the qualities "white" and "hard" in the same stone (a favorite theme of the sophists), or when one likes one thing and detests another — for example, liking life and detesting death. Consequently, one "injures" one's individual self, which is embarrassed by these disjunctions and exhausted by their weight. Instead, one should allow the vital capital to "conform constantly" to that which "comes in this way on its own,"[e] sponte sua, without pressure or even interference — as well as without resistance (as Zhuangzi puts it later, in his most common leitmotif). Thus the sage feeds his life without adding anything that might excite or corrupt it, contenting himself with "going with the flow" while being aware that the desire for knowledge is an "unhealthy offspring," contact with men is "glue," virtue is a way of "binding" oneself (excessively) to others, and, finally, the success-effect is a trinket or "commodity."[20] Since he "follows no plan," what need has he for knowledge? Since he "cuts nothing," what need has he for glue? Since he "loses nothing," what need has he for virtue? And finally, since he "trades nothing," what need has he for trinkets and commodities?

The sage does not allow his conduct to be encumbered by

knowledge, stuck in agreements, bogged down in virtues, or hobbled by success. These four negatives are precisely what Zhuangzi names (to translate literally) "the food of heaven."[f] Here once again is proof, now in magisterial form, that our terms must be made clear in order even *to be able to begin* to translate, for otherwise "food of heaven" will lead us seriously astray. Everything we have learned thus far, including the most recent point, shows that this "food of heaven" is to be understood as the antithesis of a "food from Heaven" bestowed upon us by some transcendent power — whether it be the food of truth in Plato or manna or the body of the Christ from the Old and New Testaments — to satisfy a human need (hunger for truth or love). The nourishment we are tracking is not a supplement; rather, it consists in ridding ourselves of all "supplements" who only lead us "to force life." "To feed our life celestially" is to free life from everything that weighs us down — be it knowledge acquired, agreements made, virtues adopted, or successes won — and to restore it to its sole injunction — immanence.

Chapter Four

Vacations: Finding Heaven

in Ourselves

This lesson is worth meditating on: when I translate literally "food of heaven" (*tian yu*) from the Chinese, I immediately and infallibly evoke a meaning directly opposed to the Chinese. In ancient China (from the advent of the Zhou, a millennium before the common era), "heaven" was a notion that gradually supplanted the idea of God, represented as "Lord above," Shangdi. Heaven, with its "steady" course and especially its diurnal and seasonal alternations,[1] came to embody for the thinkers of Antiquity, and for Zhuangzi in particular, the natural regulation of the great world process, which is consistent and thus constantly renews itself, engendering all that exists. The word thus denoted the immanent *source* of processivity itself, which, through its invariable reactivity to "Earth" (yin and yang), is the never-ending fountain of life. (I as an individual, however, have only limited access to it, which is why it is transcendent.) So when Zhuangzi discusses "heavenly food" or recommends "bringing (some) heaven into myself," he means simply (that is, without moral or religious inflation) that I ought to make contact with that part of myself which is pure process (natural and spontaneous) through the liberation from everything superimposed by the "induced point of view"[a] or *bias* of an individual ego. For the ego, caught up as it is in the play of for and against and in the projection of its predilections and aversions, is prevented from perceiving the world's pure injunction. The natural reactivity that renews life perpetually is thereby obscured, leaving it in confusion and embarrassment. The vital influx becomes ensnared in the "ego" and exhausts itself. So if there is any ("heavenly") "nourishment" here, it still does not rise to the figurative level, for no level of existence is involved other than the organic. Or, to put it another way, this "heavenly" nourishment is needed if I am to truly develop my fundamental organic being, for only by eliminating all encumbering affects can I adequately respond to and satisfy the vital injunction that runs through me and that comes to me directly from the immense source of reactivity that lies within the great world process as a whole rather than from the narrow orb of my desires and repulsions. I link my life directly to the source of its immanence.

With the very important contrast between "heaven" and "man," Zhuangzi distinguishes between two levels or regimes of vitality: one is the fundamental ("heavenly") regime, which I discover within me and can begin to feed as soon as my aims cease to get in the way and my causality-governing knowledge no longer interferes ("eliminate the knowledge and the cause," the text also admonishes).[2] The other is the reductively "human" regime, in which my vitality is "coerced" and debilitated by all the prejudices that impinge on it, whether they stem from desire or knowledge. A distinction must be made between, on the one hand, *stimulus* [*excitation*], which is external, sporadic, and temporary, and which impinges constantly on my affective being, buffeting or consuming me, and, on the other hand, *incitement* [*incitation*], which is fundamental and which, stripped of my concepts and options, connects me completely to the ceaseless turmoil that keeps the world in motion. Clearly, "heavenly" nourishment is that which comes from this incitement. Another way to represent the two regimes of reactivity is the following: on the one hand, when the "force" that spurs me on (ji)[b] is not well grounded or connected to the natural world process (but is instead limited to a superficial reaction dictated by my own point of view or desire and therefore weakly motivated), the expenditure of vitality within me is substantial; on the other hand, when the "force" that incites me and gets me moving is the same one that keeps the world moving as a whole and connects me to its energy, the reaction that sets me in motion demands nothing while carrying me along and vitalizing me. "When desire is profound, the force of heaven is superficial," Zhuangzi says laconically.[3] In other words, when the *stimulus* (of desire) is strong, the *incitement* that connects me to the source of vitality itself comes through only weakly because it is attenuated by its stimulative trappings. Zhuangzi neither morally condemns desire nor returns to an ascetic ethos; he merely observes that if I maintain a superficial stimulus through the use of my will, motivation will come at my own expense. It is up to me (that is, to my vitality) to feed my desire. By contrast, when the force animating life comes from the "heaven" within me, that is, when I overcome my individual perspective and embrace the natural process, I no longer need my will (I am no longer reaching out *toward* anything). The world as a whole sets me in e-motion; it reacts through me and unfolds my path before me as it proceeds.

Hence this is presumably the only behavioral choice — neither religious nor moral — available. But without insisting, strictly speaking, on conversion (since there is no "turning toward" another order of value or reality), such a choice nevertheless requires a vigorous unburdening. *Zhuangzi* calls for this constantly — I must move beyond the epidermic, personal level of motivation if I am to penetrate the world's incitement. Rather than brave winds and tides to bring my ship safely into port (my death), I plunge

45

directly into the endless flux (life), embrace its logic of concentration and dispersion, of advent and disappearance, and allow it to carry (me) along. *Zhuangzi* posits an alternative: it is either "heaven" that I "open up" in myself or the "human."[4] Of course, if I open up a part of "heaven" in myself, that is, if I descend to the radical stage of motivation at which the vital process within becomes transparent, "I then increase my capacity for life." If, on the other hand, I "open" the "human" by remaining at the level of pure stimulus and volition, that is, at the level of the artificial and the "forced," I injure and "despoil" my vitality. The only useful knowledge, then, is that which teaches us to distinguish the two levels of "heaven" and "man," as we are told at the outset.[5] *Zhuangzi* describes at length this other regime of reactivity, which is not the limited one of conception-volition but the one in which the individual being, rooted in the world's turbulence, allows itself to be transported and used.

All these formulas are emblematic of wisdom and must be read as offering a rigorous description of a fundamental form of being-in-the-world that has been stripped of the usual rigidities, obstructions, and diminutions and thus restored to its primitive intensity and raised to its full potential (of vitality). The life of the sage, Zhuangzi says, coincides with the "course of heaven," meaning that his behavior is determined solely by the fundamental process, by incitement alone, to the point where he does not need to act by and for himself and therefore does not have to "force" the life that lives within him.[6] "At rest, he shares the virtue of the yin; in motion, he partakes of the spirit of the yang." In other words, when reactivity is at work in the world it suffuses his conduct and guides him directly. Or, put differently, "when incited, he responds," "taking action only when he cannot do otherwise." Echoing the "passivity" of the creature opening itself up to divine grace (as in Christian Quietism, but without transcendence), the openness and passivity of the sage "embraces the coherence of heaven" and vibrates in unison with it. Since he is in phase with this immanence, the effect comes of its own accord, and even without his knowledge, just as our organic functions usually operate without aim or intention. From this comes an idealized portrait, another dream for humanity: the sage does not need "to cogitate or make plans." He does not need to go out of his way. "He is radiant" without glowing or burning (like fire, which consumes itself). By the same token, "people trust him without the necessity of a contract." The contractual "glue" becomes unnecessary. By "placing himself in harmony with the virtue of heaven," which is eminently natural, he is no longer hobbled by "men" or "things," by "natural elements" or "spirits." In short, he exhibits no habitual pattern, no residue at odds with his nature. "Sleeping, he does not dream," and "awake, he does not fret."

Would it be worth while to read this ancient Chinese thinker if we could not decipher, beneath the absolutized figure of the sage and beyond these conventional motifs of "heaven" and "man," the fundamental — and more common — experience that he succeeds in describing? Would it be worth it if we could not go beyond lazy equivalences (such as rendering the Chinese "heaven" by the English "heaven") and exploit the Chinese notion in its own context? Disrupting and disorienting our thinking opportunely liberates something that has hitherto remained unthought. Zhuangzi, by inviting us to explore the "processive," intrinsically reactive foundation that he designates as the basis of the real, now rescues the ideas of "getting back to basics" and "natural self-sufficiency" from the theoretical inconsistency and ideological debility in which they have lately wallowed. He gives us the concept of a true vacation, that is, of vacation understood in a way that is not solely negative (that is, not working). When we read *Zhuangzi*'s words

47

in this new light, suddenly they seem astonishingly appropriate. For is not "to be on vacation" precisely to give free rein — *throughout* our being (in such a way as to bring home the intensive force of *throughout*) — to a more solidly rooted radical *reactivity*, a reactivity that can circulate more freely because it has been stripped of its usual carapace of obligation and convention? Is not "getting back to basics" (to resort to a rather clumsy but inescapable expression) a chance to allow ourselves to be guided solely by *incitement*, freed from all febrile stimuli and in contact with a more intimate source of energy?

Indeed, when it comes to "vacations," we must concede that Westerners may have acquired politically the right to take them and socially developed the corresponding vacation "commodity," but we still do not understand what a vacation is. For nowhere in our philosophy is the concept elaborated (except perhaps indirectly in Montaigne). We still lack the "ontology." Or, rather, we lack the *deontology*, and it is precisely here that the Chinese notion of "heaven" can be put to good use. The previously quoted description of the sage's role continues as follows: it is under the sole incitement of the natural functions yin and yang, together with inner "emptying" and "detachment" (the two go together: emptying of concern and detachment from affairs), that we at last free ourselves from the reductive perspective of the "human."[7] Then, "forgetting" (an important term in *Zhuangzi*) our "focalizations" and points of view, we "align ourselves with the great natural transformation." Freeing the vital from its various impediments, we again "feed" the "heaven" in us. This formula at least avoids falling into the flabbiness and weakness of the atheoretical while at the same time refraining from constructing too much and losing the experience of the thing itself: we take vacations in order to "feed life."

With one stroke, we are also provided with a concept that outlines the fundamental relationship between the artist and his material, be it the sculptor and the stone or wood he carves, or the painter setting up his easel before the mountain (Sainte-Victoire) to which he tirelessly returns each morning. For how are we to think about what everyone knows, namely, that the work will succeed only if the artist manages to evoke a naturalness prior to both technical know-how and idea, by connecting with the intrinsic naturalness of his subject and material, which thereby become "partners" in his creation? Consider the following notions. "Openness," or "ecstasy," remains caught for us in the folds of its religious background (as do Heidegger's *Erschlossenheit* and Paul Claudel's *conaître*). "Communion" (with nature) remains inseparable from the Romantic sensibility that thematized it because it does not link up with any genuine ontology (for which its rhetorical hyperbole clumsily compensates). "Authenticity" is not based on any *ad hoc* concept of interiority capable of ensuring its consistency. "Ingenuousness" and "naïveté" are entirely too psychological. The list goes on. Western thought struggles here to express something that it nevertheless knows empirically (and, I believe, phenomenologically). All these terms miss the mark and reveal the same theoretical weakness because they remain bloated with subjectivity, having failed to locate in the creative process itself the congruence with the intrinsic naturalness of its object.

Zhuangzi describes a carpenter who creates a bell stand that amazes everyone who sees it as though it were the work of a god.[8] Questioned about his "technique," he at first denies that he has any. He goes on to explain, though, that after the incremental process of withdrawal that leads him to banish from his mind first "stipends and rewards," then "praise and blame," and, finally, "to forget" even "his body with its four limbs" and the king's court, he "enters the forest" with "concentrated skill" and "all external concerns dissipated." He then contemplates the "heavenly nature [of a tree] whose shape is perfect," and "only then does he form his vision of the work" and "set to work." Once again, the formula is lapidary but adequate: "With heaven [open in him] he mingles with [the] heaven [of the tree]." In other words, he unburdens himself of everything that weighs him down and impedes the natural process working within him — his incitement — and connects with the natural process responsible for the splendid growth of the tree. This thought is expressed phenomenologically and not psychologically: having completely unleashed his own capacity for growth, prior to all affect and intention, he immediately becomes complicit with the capacity for growth that the tree has revealed by rising so majestically. Henri Matisse offered an excellent commentary on this subject in his discussion of Chinese teaching: rather than draw by imitating as you are taught to do in school, "when you draw a tree, try to feel as though you start at the bottom and climb with it."[9]

There is, on the other hand, something that Zhuangzi does not see, something that eludes him, that his text ignores — but upon which the West, for its part, recognized and assigned a code name, a password, its ultimate identity: love (which the West conceived, incidentally, only against the backdrop of God). Let the "absolute" be not only that in which all things dissolve and in whose unity they communicate (the *dao*),[10] but also that which sets itself up in a figure and even a certain face. Let tension no longer call for regulation through relaxation, but let inspiration be infinite, and let affective force monopolize everything and absorb life completely as one consecrates (*con-"sacre*," co-"sacreds") oneself to the other, that is, to the other *qua* "other" (and not the other of the same, yin and yang). Let focalization no longer be an obstacle but that from which plenitude wells up, and let it no longer exclude but totalize. For what, ultimately, can the nature of this "heaven" that one "opens up" in oneself be? Western literature (and it is chiefly in literature, rather than in philosophy, that this is imagined) discovers this in the Passion and the gift, which are intentionally voluntary, heroic, sublime, and carried to the point of sacrifice (of an orgasmic paroxysm?). The Chinese thinker, on the other hand, envisions heaven as the full regime of natural processivity. He sees it as the refuge of his vitality, to the point of making himself invulnerable to external elements and dangers: he passes over the vestiges of shamanism in the miraculous ability to walk on fire without feeling the heat, or to soar above the world without feeling faint.[11] Zhuangzi describes a simple experience: a drunken man falls from a carriage. What is it that allows this man to suffer injury rather than death when nothing about his physical constitution distinguishes him from others? The answer is that he climbs into the carriage without noticing and falls out the same way, and "because the fear of death does not penetrate his innermost recesses," he is moved by *processive* reactivity alone, rather than *affective* reactivity. If it is true that the absence of affect in a state of drunkenness preserves us from injury and allows us to achieve an integrity of our whole being, then, Zhuangzi concludes, it is all the more true if we achieve such integrity with respect to "heaven": "Because the Sage withdraws into heaven, nothing can do him harm."

Now, the important point here is that this is the basis on which Zhuangzi conceived our relations to others and from which he drew the only elements from which morality could be constructed: if we connect only with natural incitement, we cut ourselves off from all affective reactivity, and others no longer have any power over us. By the same token, if we purge ourselves of all intentionality, no one can hold this against us: we do not attack the sword that wounds us or the tile that falls on our head.[12] If a drifting boat collides with my boat, I will say nothing if no one is aboard the other boat, but if there is someone, I will address that person rudely and move quickly to insults.[13] Conflict arises at the level of the volitional-affective self. As soon as we move beyond that stage, or, rather, as soon as we regress within ourselves to a point prior to that stage, we can get endless things from others without resorting to force, as well as prepare ourselves to counter their aggression, since they will no longer even think of confronting us.

Such are the conditions and consequences of feeding ("heavenly") life. The first case (getting things from others) is illustrated by the tax collector at the city gates who receives money from travelers without having to demand it or even ask them for it.[14] How does he do it? He "collects," to be sure, but "vaguely," without calculating or contriving. People may say that he is "dull" (for the person who knows how to keep his inner life intact is outwardly dull). While concentrating on his task, he *does not react affectively* to anyone, neither to the "violent" who refuse to pay nor to the "compliant" ones who pay as best they can. He "greets those who come" and "bids farewell to those who go," without "trying to prevent the latter from leaving or the former from entering." What does he do? Rather than withhold and spend (like those who mistakenly cling to life), he proceeds as life itself proceeds. He grasps its processivity and natural reactivity and is constantly coming and going, like the ebb and flow of the tide, like the inhalation and exhalation of living things, content to greet and bid farewell without stiffness or haste, without forcing anything and therefore without trapping anything. Thus "he follows the road that each of us follows to the end of the self," and his collections continue unperturbed. His goal is achieved without effort because he leaves it to itself, without intervening or imposing his will.

The second case (preparing oneself to counter aggression) takes us directly to feeding: the "feeding" or raising (the Chinese word is the same: *yang*) of gamecocks.[15] Here we discover a new itinerary of maturation, step by step, ten-day period after ten-day period. At first, the cock is still vain and swollen with pride, confident in its strength. Later, it still reacts to other cocks, as well as to shadows and noises. After that, its gaze is still too fierce, and the bird is still too spirited. It is ready only when other cocks can crow without provoking any "change" in its appearance. Looking at it, you would say it was "made of wood." Only then is it "fully trained," and "other cocks won't dare face it but will turn and run." Because the trained cock does not react to the other birds, they no longer react to it and have no choice but to flee. At earlier stages in the process, the cock in training was still a subject (of initiative, of feeling, of attitude), but now it is the others who become subjects for it and bear the burden and cost. It is tempting to think of this impassiveness as a moral stance, like the Stoic *ataraxia*, but it is above all strategic (here in a parodic mode). It is also tempting to think that the capacity for combat means being stronger than one's adversary and capable of beating him, but as *The Art of War* teaches, that strategy is costly in terms of energy and inevitably risky. The true defense is to be able to forgo fighting, which means not being vulnerable to attack. This is achieved not by being stronger but by making oneself inaccessible. Moreover, by de-reacting within myself and turning myself into a "wooden cock," I not only protect myself from his aggression but also deprive him of his own reactivity (the apparent source of his strength) and thereby neutralize him. He is crippled and paralyzed by my lack of response, while I am able to preserve my energy.

CHAPTER FIVE

Without "Soul"

If we wish to examine the (cultural) conditions for the possibility of thought — as I have done here — rather than at the propositional content as it subsequently develops, a remark of Zhuangzi's becomes relevant and might even serve as an epigraph for this book: "In any discussion, some things go undiscussed."[1] In other words, prior to any discussion and to the antagonistic positions a discussion may provoke, there exists — in the image of the *dao*, or the unitary process out of which all beings realize and differentiate themselves — a background understanding. The most diverse and even opposing points of view are able to stake out their distinctive positions with mutual comprehension *because* they share this background. I see such a *background understanding*, for instance, at the beginning of the *Phaedo*, where Socrates begins with the idea that the soul and body separate at death. He introduces this not as a conclusion arrived at in the course of discussion but as an already self-evident proposition: at the moment of death, the soul stands apart from the body. "It isolates itself," and the body, for its part, does the same.[2] Simmias, his interlocutor, does not think to question this. Only later, on the topic of the nature of the soul and its immortality, does debate begin. In order for such a background understanding to exist, the idea of a source of life separable from the body and relatively autonomous with respect to it must have been formulated much earlier and assimilated quite broadly. This mode of thinking is already evident in Homer, well before Plato deploys it. It is already implicit in the distinction *cum* parallel between *psuchē* and *thumos* that is developed in the *Iliad*: the *thumos* of the soldiers in the siege of Troy, the "heart" that dwells in their bosom, the source of their energy and courage, is "destroyed" and "broken" by death, while the *psuchē* or "soul," associated with the head, subsists as the visible but impalpable image or *eidolon* of the once-living being. "Like a phantom in a dream," "vaporous," it "flies away."[3] It reaches its destination "in Hades." Only later, most notably in Pindar and the gnomic poets, do we find such a principle of life implicated in perception, thought, and feeling, as life and consciousness are joined in a single entity. At this point, the soul is born as a crucial anthropological representation that philosophy henceforth takes to be "self-evident." Simmias, debating with Socrates, does not think of questioning its existence.

In essence, at any rate, the game had already been won with the opening words of the *Phaedo*, since "soul" was now in place. The Chinese tradition, by contrast, thought first of feeding "life" rather than elaboration on the "soul" because it did not establish as sharp a separation between a principle of life and organic being. It did not assign the "head" a different fate from the rest of the body and instead situated the spirit in the heart (*xin*, which is usually translated as "heart-spirit"). Indeed, Laozi urges us to shift our attention to the "belly," the seat of nutrition, where vitality is concentrated.[4] Conversely, in Plato's *Timaeus*, the head, the "most divine" part of the body, is what matters most. The purpose of the rest of the body is merely to "support" the head.[5] The fact that Chinese thought did not conceive of this thing we call a soul as a distinct entity with a destiny of its own and with essence as its vocation has enormous implications. What does it mean, then, to think, in the most general way (regarding the status of "man," his internal makeup, his fate, morality, and so on), if we cannot avail ourselves of the notion of the soul, or at least (especially since we have been wary of it for centuries now) if we *can no longer presuppose* such a notion made possible? To eschew interest in the soul, as Western thinkers commonly do today, is to ignore the residual effects on our thought that its isolation as an idea inevitably and perhaps indelibly produced. We remain dependent on these effects, no matter how hard or indeed how relentlessly we seek to eliminate them. Even if Aristotle had little to say about the immortality of the soul — and, indeed, he seems to have had no interest in it — and even if he conceived of the soul as situated on a level possessed by all living things, he nevertheless used it as a mental tool for conceptualizing the "cause" and "principle" of the body, at once *aitia* and *archē*. Consequently, the body was henceforth conceptualized only as "matter" (*hulē*) in-formed by soul. Even if it was claimed — by the Stoics, for example — that the soul itself had to be corporeal in order to exist, it nevertheless remained a distinctive principle because of its emblematic status and motive force.

The "nevertheless" I just used in the last sentence will remain permanent. Even though, since the Kantian revolution, soul has disappeared from the philosophical stage, having been exiled to discourses on faith, the notion has nevertheless found its way into technical language by way of its Greek doublet: the "psychic," whose pertinence we can hardly abandon (just as we fall back on the Greek root when we no longer dare to speak of morality and instead invoke "ethics"). With its parallel lexicons, Western thought has a convenient way of making shifts, or rather slippages and jumps, in discourse, without assuming full responsibility or justifying completely these transitions. I slough off the baggage the term "soul" carries on the Latin side or shunt it off into the realm of the "literary" so as to maintain a halo around the "soulful supplement" in compensation for the overly rigorous determinations of science. And so questions like "inanimate objects, have you a soul?" arise. At the same time, I retain its connotations on the Greek side. In other words, though I may doubt I have a soul, I will not doubt the entity I call my "psyche." A dubious operation.... Psychoanalysis itself, in distancing itself from religious discourse, may forget that it remains a descendant of this immense cultural *a priori*, this apparatus called the soul. As such it is susceptible to the same slippages as "science" (the "science of the soul," or *Seelenkunde*), which Western culture has put in place.[6] We no longer "think the soul," we no longer argue about it, but we inevitably think about how this idea unfolds in accordance with its legacy. We still think along the lines it laid down long ago. It belongs to an older, "archaeological" stratum of our mental landscape, and acts as a controlling idea that defines our epistemic axioms.

From China — that is, using Chinese thought as a theoretical measuring stick (or observational device) — we will be able to gauge more accurately what effect such a coalescence of notions may have had on the formation and evolution of Western thought. The ancient Chinese shared the idea of a separation of two distinct principles at death with Socrates but did not believe that a unique soul "withdrew into itself." Instead, they held that subtle soul*s* (plural) returned to heaven (*hun*),[a] while other, more corporeal souls mingled with the earth. The older, more monistic idea was that a human individual's subtle soul could leave the body, even when the person was still alive, and that the shaman had the power to call such vagabond souls back home.[7] This idea was clearly quite marginal to the thought of Zhuangzi, however, even though he was not far removed from this shamanic culture. Commenting on the "course of heaven" to which man returns when he connects with the natural process, he merely notes that "the spirit of the Sage is then pure" and that his "soul" (*hun*) is "not tired." Note, however, that although the "soul" is mentioned here, it is within the context of a discussion of vital potential and the conservation of energy.[8] Otherwise, Zhuangzi limits himself to various scattered designations, none of which can be regarded as definitive. Rather than being impositions of an analytic point of view, these are more in the nature of circumlocutions that play a symbolic role. For instance, he refers at various points to a "Treasury" or "Spiritual Receptacle" where worry about vicissitudes must not trespass; to the "Terrace of Spirits,"[b] a medical term, which must remain "concentrated" and "unimpeded"; more simply, to a "house," or innermost self, from which possible dangers must be barred; and, in still more elementary terms, to the "interior" of the physical form and skeleton, as opposed to the "exterior" of the physical being, about which one should not worry.[9] Let us begin, therefore, by taking note of this semantic diversity. In the West, by contrast, the legacy "soul" owes its force to the fact that a single, inescapable term took hold, even if its meaning is hardly unequivocal.

Chinese thinkers did, however, perceive in the human person a principle of animation distinct from the physical being. When it was not thinking of this principle in terms of its function in knowledge and moral perception (as *xin*, or spirit, which it located in the heart), however, it usually used the term "quintessence" (*jing*, the "refined" or "subtle") with which I began. As we have seen, it is essential that "the physical form operate at full capacity" and that "quintessence replenish itself."[10] Zhuangzi's French translator renders the term as *âme*, or "soul,"[11] but bear in mind that although it is indeed paired with the physical form, it nevertheless refers to any purified, distilled, or refined matter (the "spirit of wine," for example) and cannot therefore sustain any sort of metaphysical rupture. Associated with the notion of the "spiritual," it also enters into a more stable compound, a "spiritual quintessence" (*jing shen*)[c] that is supposed to make things "as pure as snow"[12] and "return to the Without-Beginning" rather than deplete itself in worldly affairs. It "unfolds in every direction," "there is nothing that it does not attain," and "its name is like divinity."[13] As is only fitting, no sooner does an idea of "soul" and its infinity begin to take shape than "divinity" (however loosely construed here)[d] accommodates itself to the new configuration. With a little patience, we can see something even more interesting emerge. This other possibility of thought, which Zhuangzi did, in fact, notice and toward which he seems here to take a step, nevertheless remains closed, since a short while later this "quintessence" falls back into the more rooted perspective of the vital and its organic refinement. The two terms (*jing* and *shen*) are also frequently used alongside one another to denote *different degrees* of purification, a verbal indication of their processive character, which shuts off the possibility of any form of hypostasis.[14]

There is, therefore, no such thing as "soul" (as substance, posing the question of its existence) but only a process of *animation*, which, by way of progressive purification and disengagement, leads to full vitality. In other words, the more I *refine* myself (or "decant," "unbind," or "disencumber" myself), the more *animated* I become. Thus to "feed" the "quintessence" in myself (*yang jing*) means simply (that is, without any metaphysical overlay) to sharpen my capacities and keep myself in shape. Similarly and analogously, to "feed" the "spiritual" in myself (*yang shen*) usually means to relax and rest my spirit. Although the first translation of "psychoanalysis" into Chinese was *jingsen fenxi*, "spiritual quintessence," even in association the two terms remain far too fluid and, being more intensive than descriptive, they are far too qualitative to form a stable entity upon which a form of "analytic" knowledge could be constructed by typologizing and topologizing.

Much more is at stake here than a semantic disparity between Chinese and Indo-European forms of expression. "Soul" inaugurates a whole different destiny for thought. Without a soul constituted in partnership with the invisible, we would not have been able to conceive of an intimate relationship between man and God (prayer, for example, quickly atrophied in Chinese civilization). And without a soul taking all feeling into itself so that it can reach out through the felt toward the infinite, we would not have been able to erect love as an absolute of the human adventure (Chinese thinkers conceived of love solely as emotion, or as playing a sexual role in cosmic regulation). Furthermore, without a soul splitting man between himself and his principle, we would not have been able to bestow such importance on the monologue of consciousness with itself: *Oh psyche! Oh, my soul.*[15] Nor would we have been able to celebrate the inner voice (there is no evidence of this interior monologue in pre-Buddhist China). Zhuangzi tries hard to discover within human reality an order different from that of the physical and tangible, an order in which we "keep the Original" in ourselves so as to cease to feel fear, or in which we "dominate the whole universe" and "gather up all beings within ourselves," using the "physical skeleton" as a mere "dwelling place" and taking the "audible" and "visible" as pure "phenomena" and regarding "the spirit as never dying." ... "He can choose the day he will rise [up out of this world]."[16] Suddenly we find ourselves close to the *Phaedo*. There is an appeal to detach ourselves from the sensible and a way of looking, though here only for an instant, at what might be a kind of immortality distinct from physical existence. There is transcendence here, but because it does not give access to any substantial mode of being or soul, the aspiration to surpass has no well-defined status. No doubt this is part of the reason why we find Zhuangzi attractive today. He points toward another horizon, but without raising it to a level on which the metaphysical mind might build another world. He opens up a dimension beyond the tangible and the concrete, and he does so without turning it into objective greatness or an object of faith.

In the *Zhuangzi*, there is, in fact, much discussion of amputees, hunchbacks, cripples, and individuals with hooked noses, goiters, and other marked physical characteristics. But they are raised to the rank of conceptual personages, so there can be no doubt that the discourse attempts to direct the mind to a place "beyond" perceptible form. One man is said to be so ugly that he "frightens the whole world" and is in no position to come to the aid of others who are threatened with death or too poor to fill their stomachs.[17] And yet the men in his entourage show him great loyalty, and the women in his company would rather be his concubine than another man's legitimate wife. It is reported that the prince himself, within a month of calling this man to him, becomes preoccupied with his thought. Within a year, he trusts him implicitly. Ultimately, he wants to make this man his prime minister, his only fear being that the man may not accept his offer. What is this man? The prince asks Confucius. As usual, Confucius (in the *Zhuangzi*) answers obliquely, with an anecdote: on a mission to the realm of the Chu, he sees some piglets feeding from their dead mother's body. A moment later, as if gripped by fear, they abandon her and flee. "This is because she no longer saw them," "because she no longer resembled them." What they loved in their mother "was not her physical being" but "what employed her physical being." This other thing, that which puts the physical being to good use, Aristotle would no doubt have named "the soul." But Confucius leaves it without a name, although later he calls it "capacity" (*de*).[e] In the absence of a substantial notion of the soul, this is the notion that ultimately prevails. But with the return to this fundamental category of Chinese thought comes a perspective that turns out to be not subjectivity but invisible communicative effectivity, as it flows incessantly from the *dao*, or "way," that animates the world. This is expressed in exemplary fashion by the strange influence this deformed person exercises, a currency that, though indirect and discreet, is consequently all the more potent and durable. And this is also what we encountered earlier in the guise of "heavenly" capacity — the full power of the natural process that resides within us and that we must learn to connect with in order to "feed our lives." But "capacity" is not merely that which takes the place of and dispenses with the notion of soul. In traversing the organic and sensible, it also dissolves into its dynamism anything that might solidify into a "body."

CHAPTER SIX

Do We Have a "Body"?

I can doubt that I have a soul, but can I doubt that I have a body? Or, if I decide to doubt that I have a body by making a metaphysical decision, as Descartes heroically tried to do, can I doubt that which "body" designates as a fundamental, primary notion, based on a perception that is, in principle, the most immediate and general of all, at once internal and external, and about which everyone therefore agrees without a moment's hesitation? And which it is therefore pointless to try to define because it precedes the sense of any understanding? "Body," when I say "my body," imposes its unequivocal and massive meaning all at once. Responding to the uniqueness of the soul, "body" in the West is an insular but fully adequate term that has no rival or synonym when it comes to designating the entire tangible part of the self, which it does all the more trenchantly because it compensates for what the soul, by its very definition, preserves of the intangible. It is difficult to doubt the notion of the body because it encompasses everything objective about my being. What happens, though, if the soul is no longer conceived of as an entity? Does this shift affect the monolithic nature of its partner, the body? If no essence of the soul or psychic function is posited, doesn't the essence of the body similarly lose its coherence? The consequence of this is easy to foresee: to call into question the supposedly unambiguous or, at any rate, predefinitional consciousness of what it is to have a body will no doubt disturb Western thought most intimately, more than any other point made so far, on account of the function that the mind-body dichotomy (or, to revert to the more technical Greek terminology, the psychic-somatic distinction) has in our thought (or the condition it imposes on it).

We are "well aware" of this — very well aware indeed, for it has been repeated so often — but we will not be able to measure its importance until we find a way to shake our overwhelming prejudice on this point. The conjunction of the two terms in the word *psychosomatic*, born out of theoretical remorse, merely confirms the dichotomy while appearing to transcend it. Even the concept of "drive" (*Trieb*) in Freud is a "boundary concept," as well as an "elementary" one (*Grundbegriff* and *Grenzbegriff*), and is understood in terms of the distinction between the psychic and the somatic: the drive represents, at the psychic level, the activity of the body, understood as a source of internal excitations (*als psychischer Repräsentant*).[1] The word "represent," which is also used in speaking of political representation, in itself suggests the separation of the two levels and delegation from one to the other. By contrast, "feeding life" preserves the notional unity of life and thus begins to disrupt the dichotomization of the living that had seemed such a permanent fixture of our thought. Because the phrase "feeding life" does not accord with the body-soul distinction, it not only avoids the appeal to the soul but also discreetly undermines our ability to say, analytically, "objectively," and as if the term were devoid of all theoretical preconceptions, "I have a body" or "This is my body."

The theoretical stakes are considerable. To pursue them we must, as always, pay rather close attention to language: like Nietzsche, I believe that philology is one of the most fruitful sources of innovation in philosophy. This calls for patience if we hope to get close enough. Let us begin, therefore, with the simple fact that in ancient Chinese there are *several interrelated terms* for denoting what we in the West simply call "body" (*soma, corpus*). Let us also explore the subtle differences between them. These Chinese words intersect in meaning but do not precisely coincide. Each implies a particular perspective, and these perspectives coexist side by side. None is subordinate to any of the others, and no term subsumes them all: *xing* refers primarily to the actualized form; *shen* to the personal entity, the individual self; and *ti* to the constitutive being.[a] None of these terms coincides completely with the Western notion, because each echoes certain other words, and certain pairings of the three terms help to clarify their meanings. Thus "actualized form" is understood in relation (a relationship of both opposition and complementarity) to the transcendent-animating dimension (*shen*) that precedes all actualization. The "personal entity" goes with the function of moral consciousness and knowledge of the heart-spirit (*xin*) that governs it; the "constitutive being" has breath-energy (*qi*)[b] as its partner, being the materialization of the latter by way of condensation-concretion. On the one hand, these paired terms form, as before, poles (of intensive content) rather than specifying descriptive determinations. On the other hand, when I speak of subtleties of meaning, it is because the semantic alternatives are sometimes barely distinguishable; the boundaries blur, or the components of the couple become interchangeable, suggesting shifting notional landscapes in which neither member of the pair monopolizes the meaning and no axis structures it. What is meant by "body" remains a diffuse notion in classical Chinese, and its configuration varies. Proof of this can be seen in the fact that in order to translate the modern European term it was necessary to fix a more neutral and rigid meaning by making a compound word that detaches its two terms from their semantic moorings: "body" is usually rendered as *shen-ti* (the constitutive being as a personal entity, the individual self).[2]

In Zhuangzi, however, it is the other of these neighboring terms, *xing*, or the *actualized form*, that usually carries the sense of "body" (when I say "my body"; for example, *wu xing*, "me, (my) actualized form"). But the term's meaning covers a broad spectrum, and because it has no strict limits, the notion of body thereby *seems to be graduated*. On the one hand, it is verb-like, connoting action (in the sense of giving form to and actualizing; compare *xing xing*: "to give form to form," to "bring it out"). On the other hand, used as a noun, it retains the idea of concrete, particular actualization. In this respect, it contrasts with the stage in which something is invisible because it is not actualized. Here, it characterizes the progressive (*de*), absolute capacity of the repository of things (the *dao*) — in its alternation with death, individual life is described as a coming-and-going "from the nonactualized to the actualized form" as well as "from the actualized form to the nonactualized form."[3] In a derivative mode, the term can also mean the aspect exhibited by the person,[4] or even the external actualizations and manifestations of the personal self (the *shen*).[5] In many instances, this leads Zhuangzi to clarity the notion by adding another term that pins down and focuses the meaning: "skeletal form" or "stature form" (armature) or "constitutive form with its four limbs" (or its "nine holes").[c]

Conceived globally, what I would call my "body" thus becomes here, in the language of Zhuangzi, the *particular actualization*, subject to continuous modification, which, as such, *constitutes me fully* and forms my only possible identity. Both before and after this stage of actualization, all identity falls apart: the "fundamental," that which belongs to the foundation of things (the *dao*), is the stage of the diffuse-confused and therefore also of the abyssal "blur" or "vagueness" of dissolution and the "return" to the undifferentiated. That is why Chinese thought has no ontology: it has no world of concrete essences. It possesses neither an individuating soul nor an opposing concept of matter (no *ule*, which Aristotle treats as the matter of the body). It does have, though, "materialization" by way of continuous concretion (under the yin factor), as well as "animation," which dispels its opacity and unfolds it (under the factor yang). Like the external world, I am shaped and kept alive by this tension between self-compensating opposites. The *actualization that constitutes me* (*xing*) is thus conceived entirely in terms of the process of concentration-emanation that brings it about. Not only does it give me density and alertness, but it also makes me opaque and brings me clarity. In doing so it forms and transforms me. Here, my "nature" is indeed the entire vital being heaven bestows on me before anything is added to it by my subjective affective reaction (*qing*).[d] Thus no dualism is possible here: forming a pair with the more subtle and quintessentialized stage of energetic breath (*jing*), the individuated formation that constitutes me in a more physical sense "takes root" and "is vitalized there."[6]

This, according to Zhuangzi's corpus, is how he would justify — on thoroughly naturalist grounds — not having to mourn the death of his wife: "From the mixture within the haze, by modification, there came breath-energy (*qi*); from the breath-energy, by modification, there came the actualized form (*xing*), and from this actualized form, by modification, there came life; now, owing to a further modification, there is culmination in death."[7] (I have been obliged here, in any event, to introduce some substantives as well as a temporal relationship through conjugation that is not in the Chinese, which uses more process-oriented terms.) We have here the *actualized form*, or, better, *the actualizing form* (*xing*, the only

69

word that could correspond to "body"), originating directly in the cosmic breath. It is the individuating concretion of this energetic breath and, as such, prior to the particular advent of life. The "body" does not form itself only with life. Furthermore, in order for the notion of "body" to take on substance here, it would have been necessary to envision a counterpart for it. But here the "actualized form" is that which arises out of the flows of energy that permeate particular concretions, without any break in the sequence or intrusion from without. In this transition from nonexistence to the existence of an individual person, the Western notion of the body does not figure — *cannot* figure — because the perspective remains that of a homogeneous and continuous process. This conception therefore cannot be fitted into any of our philosophical pigeonholes: the "body" is not deemed an illusory reality, and the assertion of the physical reality (of the "body") does not reduce spirit to a mere epiphenomenon secreted by the organic. Only phenomena of (energetic) individuation and de-individuation truly exist, and this physically oriented process, which is indeed the advent and development of the "vital principle"[e] in its entirety, *naturally* "retains" the (transcendent, animating)[f] "spirit dimension" within itself as it flows from the original energy.[8]

This *form of actualization*, which constitutes me, is therefore *my whole vital being* and not, reductively (materially), my "body." This becomes especially evident if I translate, as literally as possible, the way I "practice" or "put to work" my actualized form (*wei xing*).[g][9] This can have no other meaning than maintaining or feeding my life: for, as it happens, "to toil to enrich myself" to the point of amassing inexhaustible riches "remains outside" this (good) "putting to work" of the "actualized form" that I am. Similarly, to "worry night and day" about achieving honors is to "remain at a distance from it." Likewise, "concern" about extending my life for fear of death "remains far away." It should be clear why using the notion of "body" would be restricting. It misses the processive dimension, that of a global development that incorporates and is conditioned by the moral attitude, as is proper to vital nourishment. Not only does my "actualized form" (*xing*) "fail to be born" (or "to live") "without the *dao*," as it is said,[10] but also it is "by causing this actualized form (*xing*), which constitutes me, to exist (fully)" that "I can unfold my life most completely." In symptomatic fashion, translators often render the same word (*xing*), with words that have similar meanings — first as "my body" and second as "my health."[11]

Because I have attempted to maintain the broad range of the term and its theoretical implications, and because I have refused to adapt it deliberately or allow it to be reconfigured so that it accords with the lexicon of the target language (by translating it here as "body" and elsewhere as "health"), I may have drifted off course and ventured into the untranslatable. Or, rather, since I have continued to translate, my words may have become bogged down in dangerous periphrasis and become opaque. Greater fluency would ensue if I redirected the revived "body" and "soul" back into the habit (or rut) of expected meaning. This disruption of the major epistemic expectations implied by the word "body" in the West (and now, globally, in China as well) makes it increasingly difficult to trace a path from European language to that which reads so transparently in ancient Chinese. This entanglement stems from the encounter with *my* language, both its vocabulary and its syntax. But if I rework it, melt it down and reshape it, it will little by little lend itself to another form of intelligibility (since I remain at all times within the realm of the intelligible). That is, as long as I cease to see myself as a soul *and* a body, each establishing its own register, and instead regard myself as a *processive actualization* or

71

formation, organic and "functional," which is animated and deployed to a degree proportionate to the decantation and de-opaci-
fication that takes place within me. Thus we have the peculiar
form of what we would call a "life choice" as it would appear in
China: my being may allow itself to become totally materialized by
things[h] and thus become a reified thing, or else it may free itself
from these obstructions and focalizations of the vital and thus
reestablish communication both within itself and with the world,
reinciting and breathing new life into itself.

That is why the Chinese have envisaged not salvation through
eternal life but rather long life. That is also why we find that the
thought of the vital (in Zhuangzi) and the thought of the moral (in
Mengzi) fully corroborate each other. Mengzi the moralist, in fact,
favors feeding neither the body nor the soul but rather that which
is "greater" or "smaller" in myself, that which has more or less
value, as long as it is understood that both *fall equally* under the
category of my *organic being*, which is fully constitutive and, as
such, *uniquely extant* (my *ti*):[i]

> Mencius [Mengzi] said, "There is no part of himself which a man
> does not love, and as he loves all, so he must nourish all. There is not
> an inch of skin which he does not love, and so there is not an inch of
> skin which he will not nourish. For examining whether *his way of
> nourishing* be good or not, what other rule is there but this, that he
> determine by *reflecting on* himself where it should be applied?
>
> Some parts of the body are noble, and some ignoble; some great,
> and some small. The great must not be injured for the small, nor the
> noble for the ignoble. He who nourishes the little belonging to him
> is a little man, and he who nourishes the great is a great man.
>
> Here is a plantation-keeper, who neglects his wû and chiâ, and
> cultivates his sour jujube-trees — he is a poor plantation-keeper.
>
> He who nourishes one of his fingers, neglecting his shoulders or

his back, without knowing *that he is doing so*, is a man *who resembles* a hurried wolf.

A man who *only* eats and drinks is counted mean by others — because he nourishes what is little to the neglect of what is great.

If a man, *fond of his* eating and drinking, were not to neglect *what is of more importance*, how should his mouth and belly be considered as no more than an inch of skin?"[12]

I have reproduced this text in full because it illustrates the following points. First, "to nourish" is used *univocally* (vitally) and is indivisible between the planes that we distinguish as body and soul, or moral and physical. Second, the most and least valuable (the "great" and the "little," that which comes under the head of moral development *or* desire) derive equally from our (unique) constitutive being and are generically *of the same order*, like the woo and the date tree, or the finger and the back. Third, feeding an "inch" of one's skin (or belly) is *equally* legitimate. The next section confirms this: the heart-spirit (*xin*) is a "function" comparable to the functions of the senses (they exhibit the same notion of *guan*).[j] But the latter are obsessed by external things and, in their commerce with things, they allow themselves to be carried away. On the other hand, the function of the heart-spirit, which is "to perceive morally" (*si*), is wholly subordinate to my initiative. Its outcome depends solely on me — that is why the "great man" is as he is when this activity is not "captured" by others of "smaller" stature, that is, of lesser value. Thus the only moral difference between men is that some, the "great men," "follow their great constitutive being," or that which constitutes them as great, while others "follow their lesser constitutive being," or that which constitutes them as "little." The crucial difference between the spirit and the senses, between the activity of the moral conscience and material desire, is nevertheless purely axiological, because both share a common "functionality" that makes them comparable (able to be measured one against the other).

The integration of the senses and moral consciousness is such that, far from detaching us from what is supposedly a mere "body," the activity of the conscience actually reinforces this essential unity. Mengzi offers this striking formulation: "Mencius [Mengzi] said: Our [physical] form is our nature emanating from Heaven; only after becoming a Sage can one fully maintain one's [physical, *xing*] form."[13] The verb that here is translated as "maintain" (*jian*) has several meanings: "to tread upon" (as we say, "to tread a path," and again we have the Chinese motif of the "way," that is, of viability); "to accede to" (as we say, "to accede to the throne"); and "to keep a commitment" (the sage maintains his physical constitution as one keeps a promise.)[14] Or, as is said elsewhere, the virtues rooted in the moral consciousness "grow and manifest themselves," or "manifest themselves vitally," "by impressing their harmony on the look of the face"; they "are deployed over the full expanse of the back and spread throughout the four limbs, so that these appendages seize without being told to do so."[15] To the sage, the whole of his physical being becomes transparent; nothing remains to resist his injunction or create opacity. Mengzi is not content here to declare his open opposition to an asceticism based in principle; his words stand as an implicit obstacle to any possible dualism (indeed, that is why the statement is so concise). Only the sage, we are told, can fully *employ* his physique, because he has completely *deployed* his moral consciousness (*jin xin*);[k] only he can truly "practice" his actualized form and keep himself "in shape," raising his entire being to a pinnacle of intensity.

CHAPTER SEVEN

Feeding Your Breath-Energy

What blindness might philosophy suffer from, then, or what illusion might it nurse? For in the representation that it has traditionally favored of itself, philosophy not only anoints itself the queen of disciplines — at once the foundation of every discipline and the keystone of all knowledge (a stereotype now suspect even to philosophy itself) — but it also conceives of itself as a privileged activity that reflects on itself in an absolute manner. That is, it sees itself as an activity that questions itself radically and is capable of reopening every possibility because it seeks to work its way back to the origin of thought. Its classic ambition is *to assume nothing*. Indeed: unable to escape its own history, philosophy has no way of investigating its own anthropological roots or the degree to which it merely makes explicit, tidies up, and chews over certain basic conceptions (the word "conception" should be understood here in its generative as well as notional sense — conceptions both prefigure and fertilize) that philosophy in no way inherits from itself. It *cannot even imagine* the degree to which it is dependent on those conceptions. I have already insisted that "soul" and "body" are typically, and even archetypically, of this order. They are the product of more deeply rooted cultural choices — primordial cultural choices whose strangeness can be revealed

75

only through comparison with other, different choices. Why did Chinese thought not sanction a similar dichotomy in its representation of the human? Because it was based on a unitary conception of the advent and constitution of the world and of man, a more global conception, namely, that of *breath-energy*, or *qi*.[a] To judge by its ancient written forms, this Sinogram includes the element vapor above the sign for rice, indicating its nutritive function, or it appears above the sign for fire, thus representing its capacity for emanation and diffuse circulation. The formation of both men and things is to be taken as a condensation or coagulation of this continuous primal current, represented by an image that adequately expresses both the efficacy and the temporariness of the phenomenon: just as water condenses and "freezes into ice," so, too, does *qi* "condense into man,"[1] and just as ice, by melting, once again becomes water, man, by dissolving at death, (re)joins a diffuse and invisible flow of energy that wends its way ceaselessly through the world, animating it as it goes.

Atavism of thought (of *pre*thought): prior to the encounter with Europe, no Chinese thinker escaped from this notional framework or would even have been capable of suspecting its prenotional implications. In this respect, *Zhuangzi* invented nothing and merely trusted in the evidence of the ample cosmic respiration: "Human life is a concentration of breath-energy (*qi*): life is the result of this concentration, death the result of its dissolution. ... Thus it is said that what courses through the entire world and causes it to communicate is this unitary breath, *yi qi*."[2] This lapidary formula is crucial because of what it is incapable of imagining, which makes it undermine all the more radically and above all, the opposition of idealism and materialism (for us). Such a statement could easily be described as materialist, in light of its thoroughgoing naturalism (nothing beyond, outside, or radically different from the order of phenomena is introduced). But to do so would be to forget that what congeals here into a cause is not the "causalist," globally deterministic cause of bodies (corpuscles) reduced to atoms but rather a *processive* cause of breath (energy) that is self-regulated by its "spiritual dimension." Through this breath-energy, I am connected to the primordial current, the generous progenitor from which my life stems directly and permanently (as my life stems from God in the idealist vision). That is why "wisdom" (or "morality" or "spirituality" or "values": the differences among these terms vanish at this most fully de-ideologized point of the program) consists "solely" (and I shall have more to say about this "solely," liberated from the limits of any metaphysical construction) in returning to the *primordial flow*. I move back through the actualization that I am, shedding the opacification born of condensing individualization, and beneficially reactivate life through a continual process of actualization and deactualization. This *reincites* my life. More succinctly put, wisdom is a matter of freeing myself from all internal obstructions and focalizations in order to recover the communicative aptitude of the *qi* that produces me. This aptitude can neither mature nor stagnate but must be kept *alert*. Zhuangzi puts it more eloquently: "That is why the sage values the one [of the breath energy]."

Would it be worth the trouble, however, to pursue this anthropological distinction in human conceptions if the effort did not affect the intelligibility of all (common) experience? Certainly, for even if they only shakily ground themselves *a priori* — trapped from the outset in the notional prejudices that I am trying to delineate — they justify themselves *a posteriori* by establishing frameworks that make various realms of intelligibility possible. These isolated realms of intelligibility can be shaped and woven together on a single loom so as to reveal what seems to me a new transcultural and translinguistic vocation for philosophy. For instance, when *Zhuangzi* evokes the shaman's fantastic powers to move through water without impediment and to walk on fire without being burned, the explanation of those powers exclusively in terms of the ability to manage the breath-energy transforms the ancient mythico-religious sources into elements of "logic" (interpreted as *logos*).[3] Indeed, I believe that this logic seizes upon vestiges of a more ancient way of thinking in order to *elucidate*. What is it that the sage is able to "preserve," and that in turn saves and preserves him by extending his youth indefinitely? Is it not precisely the absolute source of the vital, namely, the "breath-energy"? This is the object (the least "objective" object imaginable) of the refinement and ascesis that proceed by way of progressive and ultimately forthright abandonment. Or, at any rate, it is toward such a decantation-intensification that a gesture is being made.

Earlier, the carpenter who built the marvelous bell stand worthy of a god remarked on this: my disengagement from the world and my "forgetfulness" (of rewards and praise and even of the prince's court and of my own physical constitution) can be traced back to the impulse to not "waste my breath-energy."[4] This experience is widely shared. Picasso, I think, offers the best commentary on the carpenter's confession: "Every creature possesses the same quantity of energy. The average person wastes his in a thousand ways. I channel my strength in one direction: into painting, to which I sacrifice all the rest — you and everybody else, myself included."[5] Anyone who intends to create an oeuvre should, I think, heed this motto: one's work requires one not to "waste" one's breath-energy. To that end, one must voluntarily (ascetically) withdraw from all the ordinary investments among which one's vitality would normally be dispersed; one must sacrifice those investments — immorally (or "egotistically"), as others may judge — in order to concentrate on the one goal. For it is truly at this fundamental level of the vital and its *economy*, and not, as is ordinarily believed, at the level of talent, genius, or inspiration (or, in another version, of patience and effort, all of which is merely consequential), that the work truly becomes possible and begins to develop in an unforced way. Only at this point has it tapped into its own generous source of nourishment, on which creativity depends. As alien as the two perspectives are in terms of their anthropological roots, they clearly share a common and easily identified fund of experience. Yet it seems to me that Chinese reflection allows us to shed more light on what makes all this coherent. The notion of *qi* reveals the way detachment (from both the "world" and the "self") and energetic concentration lead to the refinement-emancipation that makes my vital capacity alert and communicative, freeing it from organic encumbrances (stupidity and mental torpor) and leading to invention.

Let us not dwell, therefore, on what might at first sight seem fantastic in these shamanic tales.[6] In the account of the shaman's fabulous powers, we are told that the breath-energy must remain "pure" — in a decanted, refined state — so as to allow the artisan to free himself from all internal impediments and fixations and perpetuate the growth and fluidity of his being, to the point where he no longer runs up against the materializations and opacities of the sensible. Then he can surmount them easily (moving, according to the ancient motifs, through water without impediment, walking on fire without being burned, and so on). None of these things can be achieved, we are warned, through "knowledge," "skill," "steadfastness," or "audacity" — prowess, in short, is powerless. In the final stage, the breath-energy is no longer primordial, pervasive, and communicative; it is stiff and heavy. In this cruder stage, when the breath-energy has become dense to the point of losing all ductility, all beings, Zhuangzi explains, are confined "to the same level of phenomenality." They clash fatally with one another and men are inevitably pummeled by the elements. But the man who knows how to delve within himself by purifying and decanting his breath-energy — the one who knows how to achieve a more alert and nimble stage of existence rather than allow himself to become bogged down in the opacifying coagulation of his physical being — can recover his freely and "purely" *evolutive* capacity and thus reconnect with the ceaseless processivity of heaven ("keeping heaven entire in oneself," as Zhuangzi puts it). One who is able to do this will find himself "withdrawn" into the unlimited reactive sequence (of heaven) "whose thread has neither beginning nor end." As if sheltered from all harm, he will no longer be subject to the insipid, obtuse, local aggression of things, which will have lost all purchase on his constant development. Thus it is not my "soul" or even my "body" that I "nourish" but my "breath-energy." In the end, my internal dynamism is the most important thing to nourish.

Hence what gives breath-energy its vitalizing and nourishing power is its circulating, penetrating, and therefore *irrigating-inciting* character. On earth, we find this energetic breath in the form of winds that waft about the slightest features of the landscape and through the smallest fissures, instigating harmonious waves and vibrations (this motif is one of the oldest in China; for example, there is the notion of "wind-scene" or "wind-land-scape," *feng-jing*).[b] We also find it beneath the earth, coursing endlessly through its veins, causing mountains to rise vertiginously, tracing the undulations of the earth, promoting prosperity, and attracting geomancers in search of sites for palaces and tombs. I also find it forever circulating within my own physical being, maintaining its rhythmic pulsation in all the channels through which energy flows (and which the acupuncturist endeavors to free of all obstruction). This communicativeness of the energetic breath links my internal parts to one another and also connects me to the principle of the world's evolution and transformation: a vision at once global, unified, and astonishingly simple — indeed, impossible to grasp, owing to its simplicity. For dualism may fret and dramatize, but it also *builds*. This unitary function of the energetic breath, at once communicating and vitalizing, can only be *varied* — poetically.

Any circulation running counter to the natural rhythms will give rise to disorders both internal and external. Thus the only impediments to this circulation are the calamities of the natural world and the diseases of the individual. For the Chinese moralists, evil is nothing other than the blockage of our moral reactivity, which dulls and paralyzes our sentiment of humanity (to the point where I no longer react to the intolerable when it threatens others and I lose all "pity"). By the same token, for Chinese physicians, disease is nothing other than the blockage of my vital reactivity, which first traps and then saps my energy. But is it right to separate the moral from the medical dimension? Is not the distinction factitious, even if its effect is clarifying? In the *Zhuangzi*, when Duke Huan suddenly falls ill because he thinks he has seen an evil spirit, his counselor easily proves to him that he suffers from self-inflicted harm rather than a curse. His malady, though quite real, comes solely from the fact that his fear has created an internal obstruction. For if the accumulated breath-energy "disperses and does not return," "it will no longer be sufficient." "If it goes up and does not come back down," "the man will be driven to rage." "If it goes down and does not come back up," "the man will be inclined to forgetfulness." Finally, "if it neither goes up nor down" and collects in the man's heart, "sickness ensues."[7] From this typology, which leads to a diagnosis and clearly mingles the moral and the physical indiscriminately, it follows that the breath-energy should not be allowed either to disperse or to be blocked, either to accumulate or to be oriented in a single direction. Instead, it should be encouraged always to flow in all directions, for both our (physical?) health and the "full (mental?) form" of our faculties depend on it.

Respiration shows that the function of the breath-energy is to maintain the vital circulation within (although the respiratory breath, which is said to be "posterior," is to be distinguished from the primordial flux). Respiration is the most practical application of the vital flux and suffices to set me on the path to wisdom. Is it not, indeed, already all of wisdom? No Chinese thinker evokes respiratory alternation to denounce its inanity, as the Stoic philosopher does the moment his attention turns away from the breath that transmits life (in the manner of the divine *pneuma*): "See the breath also, what kind of a thing it is, air, and not always the same (*ou aei tō autō*)," Marcus Aurelius says disdainfully, "but every moment sent out and again sucked in."[8] Such contradictory motion is enough to reveal the nullity of the thing. But rather than see the alternation of breathing as a sign of inconsistency to be compared unfavorably with the identity of being, Chinese thinkers commonly saw respiration as an act of renewal that makes us participants in a vast movement of communication by way of concentration-dispersion, a movement that continually activates life. What characterizes the sage, according to Zhuangzi, is the fact that his breathing is "deep-deep."[9] Not only does it embody harmonious regulation in its alternation, but, moreover, the intensive implied by the repetition of the word tells us that respiration must extend throughout the physical being to the very extremities: "The authentic man breathes from his heels," in other words, to his foundations; the common man breathes only "from his throat."[10]

Various techniques employed by the adepts of long life, such as methodical inhalation-exhalation aimed at a specific organ and deep versus shallow breathing, were already known to *Zhuangzi*,[11] as were the accompanying gymnastic exercises, which employed the art of "extending and contracting" ("hanging like a bear and stretching like a bird") to free up all the difficult passages where communication might be inhibited throughout the physical being. In the Daoist tradition of vital nourishment, countless formulas and prescriptions were carefully collected in manuals, which recommended using the force of the air accumulated and held within to break down these obstructions, as well as using the "inner eye"[c] to follow and monitor the circulation of the breath so as to ensure that it brought its regenerative power to the location of the malady.[12]

The respiratory breath thus fulfills two nutritive functions at once: on the one hand, vital communication (specifically, the breath is supposed to push the blood through the veins with each exhalation-inhalation) and, on the other hand, metabolism ("spitting out the exhausted air to breathe in the fresh" casts respiration as the principal agent of vital replenishment). At times, the *Zhuangzi* begins to hint that this respiratory nutrition, which is nutrition *par excellence* because it is more refined and decanted of its materiality than any other form (though still within the realm of the phenomenal), might replace the cruder and more opaque nourishment of ordinary foods. Respiratory nourishment is not spiritual from the start (as a nourishment of the soul would be), but because it operates in a purer mode, it leads to spiritualization. Ultimately, Zhuangzi discusses the sages of remote Mount Gushi, who, as legend has it, are wholly "spiritual" beings content to "breathe the wind and drink the dew" and who, because they do not need to eat grains of any kind, are able to preserve their virginal "delicacy" and "freshness," spreading their beneficial influence without impediment or limit. Might they not — despite the suspicions aroused by what one takes at first to be an exaggeration

83

— be more than a strange fable or even a mythological symbol? (Or, turning the image on its head and interpreting it negatively or pathologically, might we not recognize here the ideal cherished by every anorexic?)

I have said enough, I think, or at any rate commented enough on the *Zhuangzi*, to show why energetic nourishment is the pivotal element in personal development. It is rooted in the most physical level of our nature and yet at the same time unfolds itself at the moral and spiritual level. Indeed, the food we ordinarily eat is already, like every other reality of the world, a concretion of the energetic breath, albeit in a heavier and thicker form. According to Chinese physiology, food ingested into the stomach is transformed so that flavors become breaths, so that the five breaths emanating from the five flavors permeate the five organs (the typologies are conveniently aligned!), and each of these absorbs the breath from its element and feeds on it. Furthermore, these various breaths mix with water and turn red under the influence of the spleen to form blood. The "blood-breath" manifests itself as ardor, whose variation with age is to be taken into consideration, Confucius warns, if we are properly to judge the ethical demands of each stage of life.[13] Moreover, according to Daoist specialists in vital nourishment (for this knowledge also became doctrinal), "quintessence" (*jing*), "breath" (*qi*), and the "spiritual" (*shen*) are the "three treasures" or three stages in the transformation and development of the personality. Breath is the median element in this transmutation. A basic saying of Daoism is: "Quintessence is the mother of breath, and the spiritual is the son." The point that there is no discontinuity in passing from one stage to another could not be stated more explicitly. The sequence can be read, moreover, in both directions: at birth, the "spiritual" enters the fetus, giving rise to "breath," which engenders "quintessence." Then, as one grows older, one must refine the "quintessence" of one's physical being so as to transform it into "breath," which then becomes the "spiritual," the most refined and vitalizing stage of energy (in which the man gifted with long life maintains himself, *shen-ren*).[d14]

Yet vital nourishment by way of breath-energy is not peculiar to adepts of long life. Mengzi also believed that breath-energy is what "fills" our constitutive being, which is normally controlled by the regulatory function of the heart-spirit.[15] This energetic breath is fundamentally, in itself, physical in nature. This becomes evident, for example, when we stumble or begin to run. For then the energetic breath suddenly takes precedence over the regulative function of the spirit and sets it in motion. At the same time, Mengzi prides himself on correct conduct that "nourishes" and ripens an "infinitely expansive"[e] energetic breath that fills "everything between Heaven and Earth" and is intimately tied to morality. Whenever dissatisfaction arises at the level of the moral consciousness, this energetic breath, which is the source of aspiration, feels the lack and subsides. Here, then, is proof, if any were still needed, that the full development of the personality, to which the uninhibited flow of breath within us contributes, is inextricably moral and physical. By contrast, the "soul" and even the "body" suddenly reveal themselves to be astonishingly abstract categories.

CHAPTER EIGHT

Procedures of Vital Nourishment

Now is the time to read one of the most celebrated dialogues of the *Zhuangzi*. At the heart of the chapter "On the Principle of Vital Nourishment," Zhuangzi brings together, as he often does, a prince and an artisan.[1] The artisan's teaching is not learned from others nor doctrinal in character, but rather arises solely from his personal experience and his skill with tools. His kind of knowledge is more fundamental than theoretical knowledge because it stems from the utility of things. He develops a mode of "understanding" or discernment, *Umsicht*, which is his own highly personal way of seeing the task and shaping his "handicraft" accordingly (Heidegger uses the word *hantieren*).[2] Indeed, contemplating a hammer tells us nothing about what a hammer really is; no "being" yields itself up from the hammer until it is used. One has to hold it in one's hand and wield it for a purpose, gradually gaining mastery of its use, in order to know it. No description can substitute. Yet a hammer is still a rather crude tool, is it not? Zhuangzi develops the theme by discussing a knife:

> Butcher Ding was cutting up an ox for Prince Wenhui. From the way he gripped the animal with his hand, propped it against his shoulder, planted his feet firmly on the ground, and pressed it against his knee,

hua emanated from him so musically, and his knife moved so well in rhythm, giving off *huo*, that it matched a tune note for note, now sounding like "The Dance of the Mulberry Grove" and now echoing the melody of "The Feathered Heads" [or, in another reading: he came down with his knife at the precise point where the veins come together].

"Truly wonderful!" exclaimed the prince. "The heights that skill can reach!" The butcher put down his knife and replied, "I am taken with the Dao, which goes beyond skill. When I began cutting up oxen, I could not help seeing the animal whole. After three years the [massive] wholeness of the animal was no longer inescapable. And now my contact with it is [decanted and] spiritual, and I no longer see it solely with my eyes. When the knowledge of the senses ends, my spiritual faculty seeks to go further by attending to the natural ["heavenly"] structure of the animal. So I attack the big spaces and guide my blade through the broad passages by hewing along the internal shape. I therefore never touch the veins, arteries, muscles, or nerves, much less the big bones.

"A good butcher changes his knife once a year, because he slices flesh. A mediocre butcher changes his knife once a month, because he hacks at bone. I've been doing this work for nineteen years, I've cut up thousands of oxen, yet the blade of my knife is still as good as if it had just been sharpened."

"Nevertheless, each time I come to a place where different parts come together, I consider the difficulty, and — very carefully, with my eyes fixed on what I'm doing, working slowly — I move the knife as delicately as possible: there is a *huo*, and it falls apart, as if it were a clump of earth falling to the ground. I then withdraw my knife and stand up straight. I look around, and when I find my inner contentment, I relax. Then I wipe my knife and put it back in its sheath."

"Truly wonderful!" the prince exclaimed. "Upon hearing the

words of Butcher Ding, I understand what it means to feed one's life."[3]

This translation calls for several comments. When the butcher says that he is taken with the *dao* and not the art or technique of his trade, the word *dao* has, I think, two related meanings: it means "the operation of things" in the most general sense,[4] and it also means a particular way of operating. Furthermore, it seems to me that this is why the *dao* is such an interesting notion. One says the *dao* of heaven, or, more absolutely, just the *dao*, when one wants to speak of the great process of things and its fund of immanence. One also says "my *dao*," that is, my own personal way of doing things and achieving success. The latter activity, as individual and tenuous as it is, is connected to the world's activity; both stem from the same capacity. Hence I would choose to translate the word here as "procedure," in order to maintain the operational and processive dimension that corresponds to the notion. It is because the *dao* retains the sense of the natural consequences of a process that it can be contrasted here with art or technique, which in Zhuangzi's usage is something that "binds" or imposes a constraint and that, by dint of routine, subjugates.[5] The butcher who follows the natural *dao* achieves ease and relaxation.

What does it mean, however, that at first the butcher cannot help seeing the whole ox, whereas later the animal no longer appears to him in its massive wholeness? I understand this as follows: at the beginning of his apprenticeship, the butcher confronts the whole mass of the ox as a stark fact. The ox is something that is simply there, filling his entire perceptual field and thus blocking a more internal, intense, and subtle perception of the animal. Then, gradually, as the years pass and his perceptual abilities grow more refined, he begins to see into the opaque mass of the animal's body and divine even its internal articulations (does this not also happen to artists, as it happened to Cézanne at Mont Sainte-Victoire?). Hence I would not translate this passage as one French translator has done ("Three years later, I saw only parts"), because no word for "parts" appears in the sentence. Moreover, the relationship of part to whole is quite Greek. Indeed, it is constitutive of Ancient Greek thought, but not of Chinese (as is well known, the Chinese, unlike the Greeks and the Hindus, showed little interest in anatomy). What the butcher sees later on, as he progresses, is neither a "part" of the ox (which implies a narrowed perceptual field), nor is it the whole animal. Rather, his deepened perception reveals the ox relieved of its opacity (which had imposed its "wholeness"). The ox has been opened up for him (as though X-rayed by spirit).

What is meant here by "spirit" remains to be seen, however. In my translation, I speak of a "[decanted and] spiritual contact" with the animal, rather than of the butcher's "spirit" or "mind," because the reference is clearly not to any organ or function (for in that case Zhuangzi would have written *xin*, or "heart-spirit") but to a *subtle and unimpeded perception*, which, as we have seen, arrives from the transformation-purification of breath-energy: transcending the stage of the crude and tangible, it gives access to "subtlety" and delves into the invisible. To be sure, the butcher does not give up on looking, as he makes clear at the end. On the contrary, his gaze focuses on the difficulty.[6] With this, the ox's body, which initially had been at the stage of perceived object or a banal presence, enters into a partnership with the butcher's internal perception, with which it evolves in concert (just as the wood of the tree collaborates with the carpenter to create a bell stand). That is why the appropriate verb here is not "to see" but "to contact." In general, to evolve at a distance, in contact as well as in harmony with things, is the distinctive trait of this transcendent faculty of perception.[a]

Last but not least, I cannot separate this operation of dismemberment even temporarily from what the prince says about it at the end, as his is the only commentary on this passage: he now understands what it means to "feed one's life." The type of activity described here can only be understood in connection with this vital question. Is it appropriate, however, to read the whole episode as deliberately metaphorical, as Chinese commentators have traditionally done? Just as the butcher initially cannot see the interstitial structure of the ox, "so, too, [the person who is learning to feed his life] cannot at first contemplate the authentic world." And just as the butcher makes sure that the muscles and bones separate at the joints by themselves, "so, too, [the adept of the *dao*] stands at the point where life and death come together" and makes sure, by contemplating his spirit, "to separate them cleanly," and so on.[7] For one much later commentator, Wang Fuzhi, the "big bones" are the big dangers and major encumbrances of life. The space between the joints are opportunities to escape from these dangers. The delicate handling of the knife at the most complex joints "serves as an image" for the omnipresent possibility of tranquillity and attentiveness that avoids any clash with the outside world. By contrast, the "thickness" of the (ordinary butcher's) knife can be our "affect," "talent," or "knowledge," which attempt to force the situation without waiting for a mature solution to emerge on its own, wearing us down for no good reason. This interpretation, which is completely intellectualized and operates solely at the level of representation, gives too rigid an idea, I think, of what can be learned only from within by wielding the implement in the process. Hence, I believe that this account of the butcher's method of operation is not allegorical but rather allusive: it *does not illustrate* the way one gains access to vital nourishment but rather *introduces it*. In the proper sense of the word, it initiates. It is not a narrative to be deciphered point

91

by point; rather, it shows how to use one's own potential. That is why the prince's very terse commentary takes a form that is not so much explanatory as indicative. It is stimulating and inductive at the same time: upon hearing these words, "I obtain" (vital nourishment).

If the lesson of the episode is to be drawn not by minutely decoding the scene but instead by grasping it as a whole, comprehending its flow and attending to its effects (such as the emulative effect of the gestures described at the beginning of the episode as a ballet), the reason is, of course, that it is not exclusively theoretical. True comprehension cannot come until I have gradually incorporated into myself the ability to remain open to change (laid out the beginning as a necessity and so magnificently embodied here). As the endlessly flowing gestures of Chinese gymnastics (such as *taijiquan*) still teach today, this is the condition that must be satisfied if we are to remain sharp and resist being worn down, just like the butcher's knife, which, after years and years of use (and there is no need to speculate on the meaning of the number "nineteen," which is formed of the figure for yin added to the figure for yang), is as keen as if it had just come from the grindstone. Thus we should "wield" our potential as the butcher wields his knife, constantly seeking the unimpeded path. For what makes such resistance to wear possible if not the ability to *circulate* and to (cause to) *communicate* through the actualized form (in this case the body of the ox) without meeting any obstruction or running the risk of becoming bogged down, even in those difficult places where the arrangement of things is most complex? There is, as Zhuangzi continually teaches us, but one way to acquire this ability: by *refining* our faculties to make them sharper and more alert.

The knife cleaves through the massive, the opaque, and the concrete because the thickness of these stages has been transcended along its blade. Yet this "without thickness" still belongs to the realm of the phenomenal; it is the extreme attenuation of the phenomenal that allows it to operate without becoming trapped in any way. Moreover, the perception of the ox is *decanted* to the point where the subtlest of internal passages stands revealed. With this exquisite perception comes the ability to guide my breath-energy everywhere, whether in the thickness of my physical being or on the scale of my life (there is no need to choose either level, and neither is modeled on the other), so that it is neither thwarted nor dispersed but *continues to flow*. The lesson is as comprehensive as can be, at once vital and moral. Where complexity is greatest, the handling of the knife (of potential) is so delicate that "with a simple *huo*" the complexity "has already fallen apart." There is no need to search or to force. A tranquil solution emerges from the minute escape route implicit in the situation itself and cautiously exploited by my perspicacity. To reach this level of mastery where an effect is produced without the slightest additional effort requires extreme concentration. Such concentration is the opposite of obsession. The procedure of following the wielding of the knife has shown how the process of immanence, by cleaving to the natural shape of the thing itself, continually finds its "way," or *dao*, without effort or resistance. That is why there can be no lesson here: immanence cannot be explained, because the thought of it is neither constructed nor theorized. At the same time there is, paradoxically, instruction (of an oblique sort), which teaches that we must learn to welcome that which comes of its own accord. This is no doubt what is most difficult: to learn to let vitality come and go, constantly, within myself.

Generally, I am rather skeptical of attempts to compare texts that come from cultures that have remained foreign to one another, by which I mean cultures between which there are no historical relationships of influence, borrowing, or contamination. Without some broad framework capable of establishing a set of questions that could make each culture aware of the other's preoccupations, such comparisons are unlikely to succeed in grasping what is truly at stake, culturally and formatively, in what I have been calling the prenotional. They run the risk of simply drawing quick — and arbitrary — parallels. Here, however, the comparison brings into view a range of oppositions too illuminating to pass up. Rather than obscure cultural roots, the comparison reveals how radical the differences between the cultures are. The passage on the workings of the dialectic in the *Phaedrus* is as crucial for understanding Plato's work as this passage is for understanding Zhuangzi's approach. In Plato, too, we find that the person who performs an operation must be capable of dividing things "into their natural kinds" and must be careful "not to ... hack off parts like a clumsy butcher."[8] Here, mirroring the "ascent" toward the idea through the conglomeration of a scattered multiplicity into a single form, is the contrary operation, a "descent" by division and subdivision of species. We descend until we reach something that no longer exhibits any internal differentiation, namely, the indivisible or atomic species, which is the proper form of the thing in question. Plato illustrates this method by using it to define love, a great Western theme if ever there was one. Within the unitary genus of "madness common to men and gods," we can still hack off a left (reprehensible) and a right (praiseworthy) member and continue dissecting in this way "without letup" until we reach an adequate level of determinacy.

Since this overall unity of the idea is comparable to the overall unity of a living creature, it is clear that such a dissection must be undertaken not at random but in accordance with the natural articulations of the thing, so as to respect the integrity and soli-

94

darity of its parts — for there is indeed "part" (*meros*). By contrast, in Zhuangzi, the internal knowledge of how to handle (the knife) is foregrounded, along with the gestural melody: the tool is not only a means but also a vector of efficacy (whether it is the butcher's knife or the painter's brush — any number of ancient Chinese painting manuals were inspired by this episode). The essential thing is to cut not so much "through the joints" as *between* them: the focus is not the *elements* that make up a structure but the interstitial *void* wherein communication (and thus respiration-animation) takes place. So the logic here is not a logic of *construction*, as in geometry, where one composes and decomposes a figure, but one of *continuation*, which allows processes to unfold endlessly. We have, on the one hand, rigorous *definition* and, on the other, *nonobstruction*, and so on. Once again we measure the gulf that separates the operation of knowledge for the sake of theory (the method of "analysis") from that which maintains and nourishes life. Instead of pairing being and thought, which lays the groundwork for philosophy, attention is paid here to the function (or the passing — "whereby things pass," *dao*) of the *vi*able.

Since immanence is not self-explanatory, it can only be introduced in stages, revealing the gradual integration of what is reflected in each case by ease and ability. This is the purpose of the series of anecdotes contained in the chapter of the *Zhuangzi* entitled "Access to [Comprehension of] Life," on which I have already commented at length. These anecdotes break the butcher episode into sequences wherein the grasp of the *dao* becomes increasingly internalized — to the point of denying that there is such a thing as *dao*. Procedural thought culminates when procedure ceases to recognize itself. The first anecdote illustrates the concentration that brings us to the spiritual stage, where the desired effect is obtained *sponte sua* and without further risk, effort, or uncertainty.[9] On leaving a forest, Confucius encounters a hunchback who is catching cicadas with a pole as easily as if he were picking them up off the ground. He admires the man's skill, just like the prince who admired the butcher's technique, and becomes naturally curious about his *dao*. "For five or six months," the hunchback answers, "I practiced balancing balls on the end of the pole and not letting them drop. When I was able to balance two balls, I still occasionally missed a cicada. When I could balance three, I missed no more than one in ten. By the time I could balance five, I was catching cicadas as easily as if I were picking them up by hand." At this stage, he was able to hold his body as still as a tree trunk, while his unused arm was like a dry limb. "He wouldn't give the wings of a cicada for all the things of the world." "How could he fail to catch them?" Thus concentration sharpens the faculties, allowing efficacy to manifest itself fully and without hesitation. That this efficacy is again characterized as "spiritual" (*shen*) does not mean that the spirit as organ is being distinguished from the "body." Everything in this episode, as in the previous one, is a matter of gesture and has to do with manual dexterity; the pole in this case takes the place of the knife. The point is, rather, that the level attained through this dexterity is "heaven," or, in other words, a natural processivity that reduces all inherent resistance and opacity to the cruder stage of the concrete. Thanks to its own impeccable perfection, it frees itself from its approximations. Once again, "spiritual" is not an analytic term but an intensive one (a suitable interpretation would be that concentration "culminates" in the spiritual).

The second episode involves crossing a gulf, and again we are told that the boatman handles the boat "like a spirit," that is, without encountering resistance, with ease, and as he pleases.[10] He, too, recounts the degrees of his apprenticeship: a good swimmer can learn the knack of handling a boat through regular practice, but a diver will already know how to do it, even if he has never seen a boat before. The lesson discreetly delivered here needs to be elucidated: seamanship is not learned by handling a boat. The knowledge required by the tool is not ultimately technique; it does not belong to the same level as its object (that is why it is no longer an "object"). Instead, the effect is to be sought beforehand, by preparing the situation or acquiring the right attitude before the fact, so that the desired outcome will flow naturally. Through training, a good swimmer comes to "forget" the element of water. The diver, on the contrary, sees the gulf as a hill, and the turning of his boat disturbs him no more than a cart sliding downhill backward. Because he has a more intimate relationship to the element, and because he perceives its internal logic or configuration better the more he immerses himself in it, the boatman wields his instrument with perfect ease. The boat is like the knife: the user who conforms to its requirements always knows where to turn.

Here, the gulf was like an abyss; there, water falls from a dizzying height — another metaphor for an (apparent) impasse, like the complex joints that impede the passage of the butcher's knife. "The waterfall measured thirty cubits high, and the rapids extended over forty stadia. Neither the giant tortoises nor the crocodiles nor the fish nor the mud turtles could swim there."[11] Suddenly, Confucius spots a man in the water. Thinking that the swimmer must be despondent and suicidal, he dispatches a disciple to try to pull him out. But a hundred paces downstream, the man climbs out of the water, his hair all disheveled, and calmly strolls along the bank, singing as he goes. Unsurprisingly, Confucius asks him the usual question, about his *dao*. The man replies that he has none. "I dive with the swirls and surface with the eddies. I merely follow the *dao* of the water and have none of my own." Having no *dao* of his own, he weds that of the water, heeding its vagaries: he plunges into the curl of the wave and lets it carry him to the surface with its swell. He can surf without a board by allowing the tide to breathe him in and out. Since he has entrusted himself to its thrust without resistance, it relinquishes its hold on him without damage. To speak in such a case of a procedure or *dao* would mean that he was not yet completely in phase with the element. It would also reveal a degree of separate, manipulative, and therefore inhibiting individuality. No fissure that might allow a subject (of autonomous initiative) to emerge in the face of its "object" is evident here. From the boat to the stream, the instrument has become the element: I no longer require dexterity or seamanship; I simply *evolve*. At this final stage, when the way of proceeding has been completely integrated, "before I can see how it is so, it is so." It necessarily *happens* this way: what comes to pass is not only "natural" but also "fate."[b] Just as we follow the swimmer in water, so might we follow a dancer on earth. We watch the dancer slide from movement to movement in obedience to some unknown yet unbreachable law that nevertheless does not oblige him to inquire into what he is doing. He executes the steps of the dance perfectly because all his gestures seem as inevitable as "fate," as Zhuangzi so pertinently remarks. He has made himself thoroughly susceptible to the pure internal logic of the process that guides him so that he no longer recognizes any separation or secession, least of all between body and spirit.

To achieve perfection through *processive induction* alone, through the assimilation of the art to such a degree that actions are no longer deliberate and all procedures are forgotten, is the way of *thrift*. "The artisan Shui could turn out [objects] as perfect as if they had been made with compass and square. His finger changed in harmony with the thing, and his mind was never consulted. So his insides were concentrated and unobstructed."[12] Here again is proof that the level of the spiritual, which transcends the tangible and accommodates the natural (and perfect) achievement of the effect is to be distinguished from, indeed opposed to, the applied and anxious activity of the "heart-spirit." Since sufficiency stems from the process itself and cannot be found deliberately, and since this same sufficiency, upon achieving perfection, "forgets itself as sufficiency," it cannot cost anything. When sufficiency is demanded from without, regardless of whether the "without" in question involves my own or others' injunctions, and when it imposes itself as a model and sets a goal for performance, it can only be achieved with an expenditure of energy. In the previous anecdote in the same chapter (which is made entirely of anecdotes that expand in many directions and link up or contrast with one another), the prince witnesses a demonstration of carriages that "drive back and forth in a perfectly straight line" and "turn right and left as precisely as if guided by a compass."[13] Since the horses are made to turn as sharply as "the corners of a buckle," it is easy to predict that they will soon tire. For in the end, the principal question is how to preserve the vital. Yet the pursuit of any goal, the quest for any end, even happiness, wastes vitality.

CHAPTER NINE

Exempt from Happiness

The point on which I have found philosopher friends most uncompromising is this: happiness, they say, clearly concerns everyone. Any other viewpoint is impossible; human existence depends on it according to Western philosophy. One could counter that truth, whose atavistic association with the philosophy of being and dependence on an expectation of revelation are well known, is ultimately the primary figure in the advent and formation of spirit. Or, that reason, in its demonstrative function and through its over cultivation, pervades the history of Western thought. Still, happiness persists as an unquestioned universal goal, for "who would not want happiness?" That people do not agree about the content of happiness is a truism that has been repeated since Aristotle, but this has in no way diminished the normative status of the idea. Thus to suppose that somewhere a certain idea of happiness did not develop, at least implicitly, is to forge a culturalist fiction that cannot withstand serious scrutiny. Thus, it is best not to try. Accordingly, what I have to say on this score has often been dismissed.

It seems to me that the thought of happiness stems from a fixation (in the analytic sense: the mind dwells on it and cannot let go). It implies a concept that, if not disjunctive, is at least adversarial (happiness against unhappiness); it hints at rupture, or in any case dissociation (between quest and satisfaction); and, above all, it is grafted onto a philosophy of finality (happiness, we have always been told, is the ultimate goal). Chinese thought dissolves this coagulated cluster of notions so completely that it exempts itself from its demands — and, I hope, will exempt us as well, in our own minds, as we become more familiar with it. "Feeding my life" opens up a possibility other than happiness, because feeding falls within the purview of a logic of refinement and transformation that develops separately from the logic of quest and seizure. As we have seen, to be "in good shape," in fine fettle, with abilities as sharp as the butcher's knife, is not to be "happy." Here we confront two different perspectives, two realms whose meanings do not intersect. When someone asks familiarly, "How's it going?" and we answer, "Fine," without having anything else to say or without needing to say anything else, there is an implicit agreement at work. A logic of passage, or of the "*via*ble," grounds the statements and does not need to be pointed out because we know in advance that our attitude is shared. The discreet affirmation is like a password, a way of slipping past a barrier, that enables us to bear daily witness to our being-alive. Speech is turned back on itself and even erased from consciousness: to say more would be to break the spell, and to speak of "happiness" would cause it to implode. In fact, it would be dissonant and even a little crude.

Zhuangzi remarks on this unambiguously in passing (by the by, because he has no need to debate the point): "Do not be an initiator of [for] happiness, do not be an introducer of [for] unhappiness."[1] In other words, the beginning of wisdom lies in reducing the gap between the two by going back to a point prior to their dissociation in order to ground them in a single all-encompassing context. This, he insists (along with Laozi), is the only way to enter into a philosophy of immanence (or of the "way," of passage or process).[2] To separate them and to grant priority to one of them — happiness — is at the same time to evoke and implicate the other — unhappiness. Similarly, to pride oneself on maintaining order is to recognize the possibility of disorder and to prepare a place for it. In this sense, "order" is indeed "the promoter of disorder," not so much because order brings disorder in its wake but, more initially (notionally), because order needs disorder if it is to make sense by antithesis.[3]

Goal and happiness have been deeply associated throughout the history of Western thought, to the point that this association has long been a tradition — it is thought's ground, foundation, ambience. Aristotle's *Nicomachean Ethics* begins and ends with it, treating it as its ahypothetical articulation, beyond which it cannot go and does not think to question.[4] In this respect, Freud followed Aristotle, freely conceding that originality on such a subject was impossible. On this point, apparently, thought can make no progress. Although the one conceived of happiness in terms of man's proper function and therefore in relation to his highest capacity, reason (so that happiness is contemplation), while the other, by contrast and in reaction, conceived of it in terms of the pleasure principle and therefore on the "model" of sexual orgasm (from which our most intense experience of satisfaction comes), both nevertheless agreed from the outset on the essential point, as if escape from the orbit of this agreement, or, rather, this redundancy, were impossible. Every art, every investigation, every action, every choice tends toward an end, said Aristotle more generally, and that end is its good. These ends form a hierarchy culminating in a single end that depends on no other and is valid in itself, autarchic, ultimate, and unique: the end in itself, which is the sovereign good, about whose nature everyone agrees and has no choice but to agree. That is "happiness." "This happiness seems to be, to the highest degree, a perfect end." Alone among ends, it is never chosen with anything other than itself in mind. In *Civilization and Its Discontents*, Freud starts with a similar premise, with no inkling that any other beginning is possible. Let us therefore begin with the sempiternal question of the purpose of life. Although it is impossible to answer so general a question in any but religious terms, we can nevertheless agree about the purpose of *our* life. "The answer to this can hardly be in doubt": men "strive after happiness." They want to become happy and stay that way.[5] No debate is possible. The point is repeated over and over again.[6] Only the rhetoric varies.

The fact that Aristotle immediately distinguishes between two types of ends, that of the work and that of the activity — where the first is transitive and leads to a distinction between the product and the operation that produced it (between the house and the construction, say) and the second is immanent and has no other end than itself (vision for sight) — changes nothing. Nor does the fact that one has to distinguish, as Freud did, between positive and negative goals, between the avoidance of suffering and the experience of pleasure (happiness in the strict sense pertains only to the latter). Once these distinctions are made, both find that happiness is unattainable yet insist that the quest for it cannot and *should not* be abandoned. This is commonplace, to be sure, but it is unshakable. Philosophy, which usually tries so hard to shun such banalities, submits to this one without a second thought. Suddenly, its inventiveness is nowhere to be found. The happy life as contemplative life is too lofty for the human condition: reserved for the gods, it is accessible to man, Aristotle says in a much-celebrated passage, only insofar as he is capable of becoming a god. Freud is more pessimistic, or, rather, he is situated at a more advanced stage of cultural neurosis. He claims that civilization, by repressing instinct, thwarts the satisfaction from which happiness derives, and, furthermore, that we desire a happiness that lasts, but when left to our own devices can experience pleasure only by contrast and therefore episodically. In contrast to the harmonious state of which we dream, ecstasy requires discontinuity to be effective; indeed, at a more basic level, it thrives on negativity. As is well known, "any persistence of a situation desired by the pleasure principle yields only a tepid feeling of comfort." What vestige of (humanist?) propriety, or what reluctance to draw too close to the flame, prevented Freud from ultimately accepting what Goethe had said so well (and which Freud dismissed with a note that it was "perhaps exaggerated"): "Anything is bearable but a stretch of sunny days"? For there is no escaping what Freud himself demonstrated: not only, as men will complain, that the world and civilization stand opposed to man's happiness, but also that man, without daring to admit it, does not *desire* the happiness to which he pretends to aspire.

It is clear that, no sooner had a Western ideology singled out the idea of happiness from the continuity of process and set it forth as "the desirable" *par excellence*, while also conceiving of it as unattainable or — worse still — intrinsically unbearable, than it became trapped in a contradictory formulation that easily lent itself to various dramatizations of "existence." Ideology no longer reflected "life" in the true sense of the word — the life of constant flow, of the discreet and fleeting, that can be said to be "going well" without cause for alarm. It rather felt itself provoked to multiply theoretical dramatizations and tabulations (which have continually injected new life into philosophy) so as to chart a vanishing line through this ideological aporia for each period — a vanishing line that establishes perspective but also a line of strength, for this tension has motivated Western history as much as Western thought. In the West, each successive generation has tried to conquer happiness anew by making a "revolution" of some kind, whether out of generosity or ingenuousness. Happiness has also been a constant source of inspiration for Western literature. Was not the novel, in particular, destined to deepen its meaning and indefatigably exploit the pathos of this most visceral of contradictions?

I find it strange, moreover, that within this framework there was no possibility of achieving distance from the broader teleology that concerns happiness. It was able to do so with natural philosophy (in the Renaissance, thus paving the way for a mechanistic physics) and, more recently, with the philosophy of history (thus putting an end to the anticipation of paradise and ecstatic reconciliations on earth as in heaven). The analysis of things more intimate and fundamental, however, remain tied to the goal-seeking vocation, which is repeatedly invoked in psychological explanation. For instance, what are we to make of the fact that Freud conceived of the "instinct" or "drive," that "borderland concept between the mental and the physical," or the soul and body, primarily in terms of a "goal"? Satisfaction can be achieved "only by some change related to the intended goal of the internal stimulus." And, "avoiding stimuli is the goal of muscular movements."[7] And so on. Leaving aside its "compulsive" character and its "source" in physical stimuli, the "drive," like art or action in Aristotle, is defined here entirely in terms of the end toward which it is directed — the "object" of the drive being nothing other than that "in which or by which" it attains its goal. As in Aristotle, we find a hierarchy of proximate and intermediate goals on the way to the drive's "ultimate goal," which is said to be "invariable." Although the idea of finality ensures that there is a logical connection between this concept of the drive (which is the psychological notion most deeply rooted in the vital) and the cult of happiness posited as an ideal end, I find the assumption of an *aim* and the overall construction surprisingly abstract throughout. There is a striking resemblance to Aristotle's nature, which "aims" and "wants" (and which is, of course, consistent with the dualist concept of the drive as a "represention" of somatic stimuli at the psychic level).

Indeed, I believe what makes the idea of process capable of a true cleavage in the history of philosophy is that it requires no notion of a goal: a process has no aim and does not tend toward an end that guides its development (in this respect, it differs fundamentally from potential being in Aristotle). Rather, it *maintains itself* through regulation; it goes on — the process continues. When someone dies, we commonly say, or, rather, let drop, "Life goes on," as though nothing else remained to be said once all arguments and consolations have been exhausted. But a process can also become unregulated, encounter an obstacle, or veer off course and end up dwindling away to nothing. In other words, a process *does not lead to* but *ends in*, and is measured by its result. That is why life should be thought of in terms of process: "*das Leben als Prozess*," as Hegel put it.[8] And that is also why, when certain Western thinkers reintroduce finality (even when they are advocates of the idea of process, which is as true of Freud as it is of Hegel), they seem to fall back into architectonic and legitimizing metaphysical patterns, which cause them to turn away from their own undoubted successes in analyzing history and psychic life.

Accordingly, it might be instructive to question why Chinese thought barely developed an idea of finality and consequently never made the idea of happiness explicit. Or, rather, why it showed so little interest in happiness. Perhaps the failure to develop an idea should count as an event in the history of thought. I recognize, however, that answering this question no doubt requires that we accomplish a very difficult feat of intellectual accommodation (in the sense in which we speak of accommodation of the eye through an automatic change in focal length), for it demands that we free ourselves from the expectations the idea of finality projects in the Western context. The task calls for patience and repetition (rather than an effort of the intellect) until the keystone that keeps our whole notional edifice intact has been removed. Only then can we appreciate the coherence of Chinese wisdom — of wisdom, moreover, as strategy. For in China not even strategy is guided by finality. One cannot appreciate any of the ancient Chinese arts of war until one understands that, in China, the ideal general has no definite, fixed goals in mind, or even, strictly speaking, any aims. Instead, he evolves so he can exploit the potential of situations in which he recognizes the "benefit" (*li*, a very Chinese notion), or, failing that, so he can exploit his adversary's potential by turning the tables on him, transforming the situation. When the enemy arrives "rested," I begin by "wearing him down"; when he arrives "united," I begin by "disuniting" him; when he arrives "with a full stomach," I begin by "starving" him; and so on. In other words, in each case I draw him into a process not so much of destruction as of destructuration (again, transformation), so that when at last I engage him in combat, he is already defeated. Success is in the nature not of a goal achieved but of a result, like the dropping of a ripe fruit. From a syntactic point of view, the relation to which Chinese thought generally gives priority is consecution (*ze*: "so that"; *er*: "it follows that"; and so on).[a] Chinese lacks the range of cases and the panoply of prepositions that broaden the spectrum of finality in Greek. In notional terms, moreover, Chinese thought is familiar with the motif of the target and aiming at the center (*zhong*). It also recognizes the design and the map (*tu*).[9] At times it even resorts to the idea of an objective of action (*di*, especially in legal thought).[b] Yet it did not develop any of these notions into coherent explanatory concepts.[10]

Further proof of this assertion can be seen in the fact that it was necessary to translate "goal" into modern Chinese (as *mudi* or *mubiao*)^c in response to the West. In place of the Greek preoccupation with *telos* and finality, Chinese thought emphasized what I have called *being in phase*, with success measured not by conformity to some aim but rather by the capacity to induce forgetfulness. "A shoe is adequate if it makes us forget the foot. A belt is adequate if it makes us forget the waist.... Let adequacy begin and nonadequacy cease and you achieve the adequacy that makes you forget adequacy."[11] Instead of the idea of destination, Zhuangzi offers that of "free evolution" (*you*),^d proceeding in comfort, at will, without a designated port and without anxiety over the outcome. Yet might there not be some ambition or will to attain? In the *Zhuangzi* we read these words of Confucius's: "Fish go [tend] among themselves in the water; men go [tend] among themselves in the *dao*. Since fish tend among themselves in the water, it is enough to dig a pond, and they will find nourishment; since men tend among themselves in the *dao*, it is enough to stop bustling about, and life will decide."[12] Here, "to tend" means to become absorbed in myself and forget my destination; instead of "going toward," I "go among" (*xiang*: a fixed *direction* gives way to carefree *evolution*). Far from thinking of the *dao* as a way that *leads to* (truth or wisdom or what have you), human beings swim in this milieu of endless movement, going around and around as easily as "fish in water" — the triviality of the image, in the Chinese language as well as in our own, speaks volumes about how unproblematic it has become. It allows us to see that once we have given up goals and the burdens that go along with them, *life itself* decides how it will go. Once freed of all impediments, life itself is capable of inducing and inciting, so that the result flows constantly and consequentially to the point of satiety. There is no need to project the result some distance away (necessitating a quest) or to turn it into a fixed finality.

The absorption of finality into a logic of consequence led to a reduction of the idea of happiness. True, we find a notion of felicity in the form of favor bestowed by heaven or by one's ancestors in the most ancient Chinese thought. Yet even when it is said to be "limitless" and associated with the royal mandate, this felicity is essentially material in nature, taking the form of rank, honor, or prosperity (see the notions of *fu*, *lu*, and *xiu* in the *Shijing*).[e13] We also find this in celebrations of the New Year: "Lots of money, lots of children." In this sense, it is close to what the Greek *eudaimonia* was initially: the "good share" or "good daimon" awarded by the gods. Here is yet another occasion to observe that the gap between different civilizations is found not so much in their penumbral origins as in the theoretical divergence that occurs as thought reflects upon itself and justifies its own constructs. In the Greek world, the idea of happiness eventually broke away from the idea of felicity bestowed from without by superior powers in order to take on a deeper significance in the "soul," which became the medium of its demands. For Heraclitus, it was each man's own character, his *ethos* that became his daimon and made him happy or unhappy.[14] For Democritus, happiness (as *eudaimonia*) "is not constituted of flocks or gold"; rather, the soul is its "dwelling place."[15] The construction of the notion would end with the constitution of the various parts of the soul and the assimilation (in Plato) to *thēoria*, upon a foundation of finality. From then on, of course, the Greeks held fast to happiness as the universal end, because ultimately they could not imagine man tending toward anything else — indeed, they could not imagine him as not "tending toward" (*ephiesthai* followed by the genitive: the verb with which the *Nicomachean Ethics* begins) something. Have we followed in their wake? They imposed this axiom on the Western mind so thoroughly we have forgotten how much this *existential construction* of happiness owed to a peculiar syntax, a syntax of ascription and subordination, whose resources their construct exploited. The structure of ancient Chinese, which is formulaic and not much indebted to syntax but embellished by effects of parallelism based on the polarity of yin and yang, gave rise to an interplay of correlations and alternations that led to the expression of constant variation within a process, and consequently to a concern for *vital evolution*.

The question, however, cannot be circumscribed simply by exploring the vicinity of the associated notion. It has many branches and opens up fissures that strike deep into the ground of thought. Is it possible to conceive of human ideals without a concept of finality? *Zhuangzi* examines a range of ideals, from the ascetic rejection of the world to the full embrace of long life. Some "delve into the spirit in pursuit of more noble conduct," withdraw from the world, adopt eccentric manners, and complain and vituperate in the name of principle. These hermits of the mountains and lakes devote themselves to "desiccation through asceticism" or to "drowning themselves in the gulfs." Others "contemplate humanity," "equity," and all the moral virtues as they seek to perfect themselves: they are devoted to ensuring the peace of the world and to "teaching course after course to their schools." Still others "speak of exploits and seek to establish their reputations"; they determine the rites to be observed by princes and vassals and tell people how to behave in the highest as well as the lowest society: they are devoted to "ensuring that order reigns in the world" and "to honoring their prince and strengthening the state." Others "haunt ponds and swamps" and like to fish in solitude, shunning all occupations: these "guests of the rivers and lakes" are devoted to "enjoying idleness." Finally, there are those who devote themselves to breathing exercises and practice gymnastics to achieve longevity: they are dedicated to "nourishing their physical form" and "growing as old as Pengzu."[16]

111

Two important figures are missing from this review of ideal lives: the philosopher and the priest. Neither the desire for knowledge nor the mystical vocation is considered; contemplation and the contemplative life are not mentioned. Note, too, that these various lives are presented in parallel rather than arranged hierarchically; no aspiration is said to prevail over or dominate any other. In particular, the last two types — the carefree and unoccupied life in nature and the pursuit of long life, which usually define the limits of the Daoist tradition — are granted no priority. The ideal is not detachment from or superiority over others. Nor is it to promote a superior end taken as a token of the destination toward which we are headed. There is no *construction of ends* oriented toward some ultimate end. Where, then, might the position of the sage be in this panoply? He has no designated place, no fixed and invariable position that would allow us to characterize him. Nor does he occupy some other place not mentioned here. *Zhuangzi* reproduces the list, systematically maintaining the acquired benefits while denying the functional objective, and in doing so he shifts from the logic of finality to that of consequence. Concerning the sage, it is said: "Without having to delve into the spirit, he has a lofty life; without having to study morality, he perfects himself; without having to accomplish great deeds, he causes order to reign in the world; without having to live by a river or an ocean, he enjoys leisure; without being obliged to perform respiratory gymnastics, he achieves long life."[17] He benefits from all these possibilities at once, achieving the result without having aspired to it. He does not aim at any of them and is therefore not limited by their incompleteness. The solution is not one of synthesis but of relinquishment, and thus obtaining without striving: "In all of this there is nothing he does not give up, yet there is nothing he does not have."

Just as "superior virtue" does not seek to be virtuous, which is why it never falls short of virtue (whereas "inferior virtue," which seeks virtue without end, is never more than virtue narrowly construed),[18] the full effect here is free to come about because the sage does not make a goal of it. "Gentle and detached, he does not incline one way or the other or become stuck in his way, which is therefore endless, and all good follows him." The mistake that all others make is to remain "attached." Not only do they limit the range of possibilities from the outset by choosing priorities, but their *attachment* also creates a clenching-fixation that diminishes the ability of the effect to come *sponte sua*. Only when an effect is not sought can it flow in all its fullness; only then can we allow it to *proceed*. We must not cling to carefree idleness if we wish to enjoy a happy insouciance. By the same token, it is pointless to dedicate ourselves meticulously to the practices of long life if we wish to achieve longevity naturally (there is no need to "take" vacations — as we are wont to say, as if what we anticipate so eagerly could be seized — if we wish to be on vacation in our spirit, and so on). The moment we take the effect as the object of a quest (singling it out in order to make an "object" of it), the moment we take it as our goal, we are reduced to grasping it, which is not only costly but also invariably disappointing, owing to its limitation. Happiness becomes *unattainable*, because it is always pushed farther into the distance, or it becomes *unbearable*, simply because grasping it destroys its value as an end still capable of inspiring desire.

The "floating" word admirably expresses this ability to avoid focusing on any goal so as to allow ourselves to be borne along by never-ending effect: "His life is like floating, his death like resting."[19] Here, "floating" is not a sign of the ephemeral or the threat of inconstancy, much less of insubstantiality. In this respect it differs sharply from the "floating world" depicted in Japanese *ukiyo-e* engraving, which captures life's fugitive, rare, and painful charm. Floating is the ability to avoid getting locked in any one position or tending in any particular direction. It means to be in constant motion, susceptible to the ebb and flow of respiration, without incurring expense or risking resistance of any kind. The word "float" negates all thought of a destination and therefore cancels out any idea of finality, thus contradicting better than any other word the aspiration to and quest for happiness. It expresses better than any other the maintenance and nourishment of the vital. To float is to designate no port and set no goal, while maintaining oneself in an emergent state — alert and unencumbered. It is not the vagueness of hesitation, ambivalence, or drift (or the adventurous intoxication of the unguided, as Rimbaud would have it). Boats that float easily at anchor in a bay undulate with the waves and can animate a landscape. "To float," with its connotation of availability, stands in contrast to the drama of crossing (confronting perils that end in death: what meaning has such a voyage?) and the torpor of immobility (the morbid eternity of a world of essences). "To float" is not to advance toward or to stand frozen but to move and to change at the world's behest: "The nature of water is such that when it is not troubled, it is clear, and when it is not moving, it is flat; but when it is held back and does not flow, it can no longer be clear."[20]

Extending the connotations of "flotation," "clarity" avoids both agitation and nonreplenishment, turbidity and rot. There is neither precipitation nor stagnation, and if there is no tending toward anything, there is no holding back. Clarity, whether in water or in the realm of the vital, comes from calm flow and ease of passage, from movement that is unforced as well as unimpeded. It comes from fluidity alone. "There is movement, but along a natural ('celestial') course, and this is the way to feed one's spiritual dimension (*yang shen*)." Here, of course, "spirit" does not

mean an entity opposed to the body but refers to an endless unfolding of one's abilities by way of refinement. As we have seen,
the expression commonly refers to calm relaxation as a means of
fully exploring one's faculties, just as water that is not agitated
flows smoothly and clearly. Tension comes from having a goal: by
relinquishing this goal and the tension that comes from striving to
achieve it, we open ourselves to the flow of the vital, which constantly clears and purifies, stimulating and replenishing life.

Adequacy is necessary if the inner relaxation and contentment
that nourish vitality are to be achieved, but how are we to understand "adequacy" if there is no goal? What sort of adequacy can
there be in floating? A passage in the *Zhuangzi* puts us on the
right track by rejecting the answer we expect: "He regrets nothing when he goes too far; when he performs adequately, he takes
no credit."[21] We expect the opposite — that the sage will experience "regret" when he goes too far and exceeds the limit or
misses the target. Indeed, the passage was misinterpreted in this
way by commentators who believed that the sage must perform
adequately in every situation. But other commentators encourage
a more literal interpretation: if the sage has no regrets when he
goes too far (and does not congratulate himself when he hits the
mark), it is because he has no aim of his own, and hence no opportunity to seize it, and is therefore in no danger of failing to do
so. The *kairos* structure disappears for him; the adequacy/inade-
quacy distinction no longer holds, not because he transcends it
but because it no longer makes sense. Since he is "floating," he is
no longer responsible for whether he hits the target or not, so he
no longer deserves blame or credit. All he does is respond to the
incitements that move him, and since these come from the world's
flux and play a role in its replenishment, there is no longer any
reason to ask whether they are justified. At this stage (extinction
of all autonomy), responsibility and loss are no longer possible:

Leave a boat in a ravine or a mountain in a valley: one can then say that it is in a safe place. Yet a strong enough person could still come in the dead of night and carry [it] off on his back without attracting the attention of those who are asleep. When the small is placed in the large [or "the small as well as the large"], it fits, and yet still it may be lost. But when the whole world is placed in the whole world, so that [it] cannot escape, all the conditions of an unchanging reality are met.[22]

At this stage, "the sage evolves at a level where nothing can escape and everything exists." He "finds good in early death" as well as "in death in old age." He appreciates the beginning as well as the end and experiences no sense of lack or failure. Wisdom consists in expanding the range of things where distinctions between adequacy and inadequacy and between happiness and its opposite no longer apply, so that the whole world appears as a process "involving countless transformations that have no end."[23] The "incalculable joy" of achieving this would, in fact, be rather banal if it involved a mystical vocation and there were a God to authenticate the feeling of plenitude. Here, however, there is no reference to another world. Indeed, no trace remains of a world behind the world, like the one beyond all the cosmic cycles that still haunts Stoicism. It is enough to "place [or lodge] the world within the world" (or, more precisely, the "under heaven" within the "under heaven"), for there is no place here for anything like absence or, consequently, a quest, which any end worthy of aspiration must subsume. Put another way, the sage "lodges" realities "in their uses"—he restores them to their common vocation of "communicating" and "passing"[f] and thus makes them "opportune."[24] He gives them shelter, as one finds lodging for a guest at an inn: although the arrangement is temporary, the fundamental relationship remains the same. He accompanies them in their transition, which is therefore identified as processive rather than ephemeral. The transitional is thus not impermanent but a useful element in the vast "operation" of things (*dao*).

To be sure, the word "useful" is still too laden with finality, too stoic, too remote from the versatility of things that *evolve*. To express what we are calling the "constancy" of countless transformations, it is better to rely on a certain alternating parallelism of expression which imitates the motion of a transition without beginning or end, eschewing both the enigma of the beginning and the drama of the end: "Encountering, he does not oppose; surpassing, he does not hold on."[25] The sage welcomes but does not cling. These phrases artfully express the avoidance of two extremes, saturation and exhaustion, each leading inevitably to the other, wherein lies the source of the tragic. So long as transition sustains itself without flagging, life persists in the endless flow: "He takes in without filling himself; he draws out without emptying himself."[26]

If there is a common motif in the religious sphere, surely it is that of the soul as mirror, the idea that the pure and pacified soul can reflect by recording within what Gregory of Nyssa calls "the images and forms of virtues exhibited by God." From its earliest occurrences in Plato and Plotinus to its magnification in the writings of the church fathers, the mirror was honored for its ability to represent truth faithfully (if passively) while also partaking of the divine. In a celebrated study, Paul Demiéville distinguished two functions of the soul's mirror: to demonstrate the unreality of the phenomenal world, and to stand as a symbol of the absolute.[27] Demiéville's broad comparative approach finds thematic links among the thinkers of India, the Chan, the Arab world, and Christianity. In *Zhuangzi*, however, the mirror finds no such mystical employment and is understood in an entirely different way:

"The accomplished man uses his spirit as a mirror: he does not accompany [things] or anticipate them, he responds to them without hoarding. That is why he uses up the things [reflected in him] without being hurt by them."[28] The virtue of the mirror is that it accepts but does not hold: it reflects *everything* it encounters but allows things to *pass by* without clinging to them. It does not reject or retain. It allows things to appear and disappear without clinging to them. That is why its capacity can be used endlessly without ill effect. Indeed, the mirror symbolizes the way a thing can serve as a passage while retaining its capacity and never wearing out.

CHAPTER TEN

On Hygiene; or, The Desperate
Desire to Endure

When, after a protracted agony, the political and social structures of the Chinese empire collapsed in the late second century at the end of the Han dynasty, individuals were left with virtually no refuge from recurrent outbreaks of violence and the exactions of despots other than to withdraw into themselves. "Feeding one's life" became a primary theme of meditation for many literati. Xi Kang, one of the most fascinating personalities and most brilliant and cultivated minds of the third century, chose the phrase as the title of his principal essay.[1] Centuries after Zhuangzi, he returned to his teaching and elaborated on it in his reflections on longevity. As Donald Holzman writes in his introduction to Xi Kang's thought, he understood the phrase "to feed life" in "the richest and most varied way: to feed the body, to feed the spirit, to feed the soul; ultimately he was concerned with the quintessential problem of religion, and the goal of Hi K'ang [Xi Kang] was his salvation, his 'Long Life,' as he puts it, his eternal life."[2]

Without denying in any way the fact that "feeding life" is one of Xi Kang's central concerns, I believe that the example of the sentence above suffices to show the extent to which the theme loses its distinctive meaning, which is diluted and distorted as soon as the European ideas ingenuously listed here are deployed as if there could be no question of their relevance: the "body," the "spirit," the "soul," the "religious" (posed, to be sure, as a "problem"), to say nothing of the "goal" of "salvation" or "eternal life." Indeed, I find the case enormously instructive, and valuable as a warning. The Western sinologist has here laid bare our entire theoretical panoply in a single sentence, and, having done this, he is immediately caught up in a series of deductions over which he exercises no control, which inevitably take him farther and farther from the thought on which he claims to be commenting. Once "body" has been posited, its companion "soul" appears next to it; the "religious" emerges as a level of analysis required for the articulation of these two notions; "problem" and "goal" face off (because when existence is conceived as a problem, we begin to set goals for ourselves), with the tension between them defining the field of thought; and, ultimately, the only (logical) way out is "salvation." How could "eternal life" not be invoked in the end as the legitimate culmination of all hope? Yet ancient Chinese thinkers did not think in terms of eternity (associated with being) but of the "endlessness" of duration, and, as the commentator Holzman himself states, the Chinese thinker spoke not of eternal life but only of "long life." Thus we see how a coherence has been superimposed on the material without the European commentator's even noticing — a coherence that projects our expectations and reestablishes the European ideological and intellectual matrix, which constitutes a system, or a habit. It is the very habit that my entire text up to this point has sought to destabilize, or from which I have patiently endeavored to escape and open up a new avenue of thought. Until we begin — locally — to decategorize and recategorize, and cease to believe that we can use (especially) our most general ideas, we may think we have traveled when in fact we have not left our armchairs. Otherwise, to alter the metaphor, when we pull up our nets, we find nothing in them but known species, "existential" ideas with which we are already familiar.

Chinese thinkers, meanwhile, have elaborated an alternative framework for thought. Some say that immortality can be achieved through study. In other words, we need not die. By contrast, others say that nowadays the longest life span is no more than 120 years, as has always been the case. The idea that one can live longer than that is myth or madness. "These two positions depart from reality." For on the one hand, unless we have seen immortals ourselves, it is possible to believe in their existence only if we trust the reports of those who claim to have seen them. Clearly, such beings must possess an energetic breath very different from our own because longevity is natural to them, rather than something obtained through study or diligent application. (Since the quest for immortality does not concern us, let us set it aside.) On the other hand, if we "direct and nourish" our own breath energy, we acquire an ability to adapt to the logic of the vital and thus to make full use of the vitality that has been imparted to us. In this way, we can live "at best some thousands of years and at worst some hundreds." The question then becomes how best to *prolong one's life*, since the possibility of doing so depends entirely on how we manage things. Why do most men fail in this enterprise? Because they are not sufficiently attentive to the subtle ways in which they deviate from their ambition. They fail to understand that our vital potential can produce a larger or a smaller yield, in the agricultural or financial sense: a good field is said to yield ten *hu* per *mou* of land, but if one cultivates the land more intensively by dividing it into smaller parcels for the sake of better irrigation, a yield ten times greater can be achieved. Similarly, market transactions can be made to yield many times the usual profit. Though such extraordinary results may be surprising, they are not fantastic hopes but straightforward consequences of the art of management. Why shouldn't we manage our vital potential as we would any other form of *capital*, since we know that capital is something we are bound to squander unless we learn what it takes to make it productive?

"Feeding one's life," the phrase used to translate our traditional notion of hygiene in China today (*yang-sheng-fa*),[a] is nothing other than this art of management. Before the word "hygiene" became associated with public health (and even security in the wake of an expanding science of disease), it had a more primary, private sense, yet the European concept still strikes me as relatively impoverished compared with the Chinese one. In any case, it appeared only in the great medical treatises of the ancients, and even there it occupied only a small place and did not intersect with the concerns of the philosophers. Greek thinkers as ancient as Plato were able to define health, but it never occurred to them to make the art of preserving health and prolonging life the principal axis of their philosophy. The primary concern of Western medicine has, of course, been to explain and treat illness. Its foundation is anatomy, and its practice culminates in surgery. It is extremely interventionist. One has only to listen to its contemporary vocabulary, which is almost traumatic in its bluntness: the surgeon "operates" on his patient; the physician tells us to submit to "a minor procedure." By contrast, Chinese medicine is founded on its pharmacopoeia. Chinese doctors scarcely distinguish between nutriments and drugs, see no discontinuity between therapy and geriatrics, and prescribe substances primarily to promote longevity, secondarily to enhance vital energy, and only thirdly for therapeutic purposes. Chinese medicine is said to be "soft," as opposed to Western medicine, and the emotional overtones of this simple adjective serve to define a genre. Surgery is invoked only as a last resort, after gymnastics and massage, dietetics, rules of life, breathing exercises, and visualization practices (that enable us to keep an eye on "spirits" in the body).

In his reflection on "feeding life," which is indeed at the heart of his thinking, Xi Kang attests to the foregoing in two ways. In his discussion of remedies, he mentions only the superior category, which "nourishes our lot of vitality," and the intermediate category, which "nourishes our nature." (The two inferior remedies, acknowledged to be toxic, are traditionally assigned the role of treating illness.) In addition, Xi Kang recommends preliminary action to alter conditions: one should take steps to prevent disease and weakness so as not to have to "intervene" more substantially at a later stage. (The same principles are at work in Chinese arts of strategy, according to which the enemy must be defeated before he is attacked and, indeed, in order to forestall any need to attack him.) This should be done while we are still healthy, before the first symptoms of decrepitude appear. Once the process of weakening begins, Xi Kang notes, its effects accumulate progressively: first "decline," then "whitening," then "aging," then "decease" — all of which happens without our noticing, as if it had no "beginning."

Such an evolution might be thought "natural," or we might complain of the moment when the malady first struck us, without noticing the "accumulation of dangers" that occurred prior to its appearance. If the major mistake is thus to take "the first day we feel ill" for the "beginning of the illness," it becomes legitimate, in contrast, for the art of "feeding life," if developed to the utmost, to deliver us from therapeutic obligations. If the affliction of an organ is merely the ultimate stage, we need never resort to surgery. It becomes the physician's task to promote health rather than care for disease, just as it is the peasant's task, according to Mengzi, to assist in the (natural) process of growth by hoeing the soil in which shoots are rooted rather than pulling them out of the ground to make them grow (or standing by the side of the field, content to watch).[3] There will be no reason to oppose art to nature, *technē* to *phusis* as the Greeks did (or even to understand *phusis*, as Aristotle did, by taking *technē* as the model). To borrow an expression from Laozi (for the idea of processivity is most general in China), what is necessary is not "to dare to act" but rather to "help that which comes about by itself" ("of its own accord"). In other words, we must help life come to life, as it is inclined to do on its own, just as the plant is inclined to grow.[4]

The question of hygiene's place and significance would seem secondary, or in any case insufficiently noble in the eyes of philosophers, if it did not reveal something of far greater importance about an epistemological order, touching on the unspoken assumptions that precede all thought. In this instance, those assumptions have to do with a question that might nevertheless seem more immediate and less constructed: not what life to choose, which is already very abstract (because philosophy since Plato has been very fond of assigning roles), but how to organize, or, rather, "manage," one's life. If we approach it from the angle of managing the vital, the thought of life is accessible in a more elementary, more rooted, less projected way than it is in morality or religion. Once broached, the question of hygiene can serve as a powerful theoretical instrument, because it helps to reveal what pattern of notions and ideas encouraged its development in one tradition and what other pattern obstructed it in the other. What complex but logically interrelated approaches were driven by the implicit assumptions of Chinese thought to the point where they became central to the reflections of a man of letters like Xi Kang, while other theoretical orientations blocked the way in Greece and turned philosophy's attention in other directions? When we follow the common theme of "self-control" or "self-governance," which formed the basis of traditional hygienic thought in Europe while it was being broadly developed in China, a point of contact between the two cultures appears. This point of contact has less to do with the concepts themselves as with something more fundamental — the perspectives and *ordering functions* from which the concepts are derived.[5] And since a perspective can only be reflected in the gaze of another, I speak here of hygienic thought as an *instrument* that *reveals* what cannot otherwise be seen.

The Greeks *thought of defining* health in many domains, particularly in the conception of the city. They did so in terms of the just: just mixture and just measure (Aristotle), or, Galen added, just measure of the homogeneous elements of bodies and just symmetry of its heterogeneous parts. It was a *constitutional* relation of parts to whole that served as a paradigm for all Greek thought, recurring homologically in discipline after discipline: in grammar and rhetoric, we find words made of letters, sentences of words, periods of sentences; in geometry, we find lines made of points; in physics, we find corpuscles made of atoms; and so on. The same is true of health and of the city. The master notions of ancient and Renaissance theories were thus *complexio-compositio-unitas*: "complexity," just "composition" in form, size, and quantity, and "unity" are coequal notions. Every malady consists in a disruption in one or more of these dimensions. Consequently, the Greeks conceived of health as their sculptors and painters dreamed of the canonical beauty embodied in the nude (the art of the nude rested essentially on the integral relationship of parts to whole). Galen himself, following Polyclitus, set out to find a principle common to the simple and the composite. This led him to conceive of the fabrication of the living in ideal terms as a creation of beauty — at least until his thought reached its limit and foundered in the aporia of the formless, which he discovered in *On the Formation of the Fetus*.[6] Once again, it was the idea of the model that prevailed in Greece. It became the source of the West's theoretical strength, and was consecrated in mathematics (the model of the model), to the point where a distinction was drawn in between *model health* and *real health*, or between absolute health and relative health. This allowed some latitude between health as it was conceived of (paradigmatically) by philosophers and health as it was studied (pragmatically) by "physicians." This divorce had important consequences. Can absolute health be experienced? Or does it condemn one to "eternal suffering," as Galen already perceived, because it is inevitably posited as unattainable (in which case it is akin to "happiness" conceived as an ideal end).

Turn to the beginning of Celsus: you will find that the thesis of his first book of medicine — which is devoted, in accordance with the teachings of Hippocrates, to the man in good health, *sanus homo* — fails to cohere because it lacks an overarching concept that ties it together, sets things in order, and justies its message. Celsus draws his method essentially from rhetoric: the praise of *varietas* (*modo ... modo*: "to be now in the country, now in the city," "sometimes to partake of a banquet, sometimes to abstain," and so on). But this method of variety lacks a foundation in a logic of regeneration through alternation, as in China. The structuring arguments are those of just measure (sexual relations are "not to be indulged in to excess or unduly avoided," and so on) and attending to the particular, as opposed to general principles (the mode of life is to be modified according to age, constitution, season, and so on). Otherwise, the text lapses into an insipid recital of truisms: "When one has digested well, one can rise without danger"; "One should sometimes do more, sometimes less"; and so on. In heaping up so many banalities, the discourse actually becomes interesting, precisely because it raises the question of the *uninteresting*: What, in the West, is a discourse that *is not constructed*? Because abstraction fails to define health, and health cannot be apprehended within a system — these being the two major theoretical moves we learned from the Greeks — what we are left with is a text condemned to reel off a miscellaneous assortment of prescriptions and recipes, a tedious inventory that has nowhere to go.

By contrast, what notion lies at the heart of Xi Kang's essay, influencing all his reflections and leaving its mark on Chinese thought in general? I would translate it as "structure" or "internal coherence" in the "development of the vital" (*sheng-li*),[c] since everything involving health and longevity depends on the ability not to deviate at all from the *coherence* needed to maintain life. Before being used in the modern era in a limited, scientific way to render the European word "physiology" into Chinese, this notion served to tie medicine, hygiene, and philosophy together in a single whole. The Chinese also conceived of health as equilibrium, but, as always, they understood this equilibrium in terms of an ongoing process (rather than a mathematical calculation or proportion): not as a norm of the just, with archetypal value, but as that which allows the course of the world or of life to maintain itself, and thus to endure, through alternation and compensation modeled on the course of heaven. The principle of internal coherence in the development of the vital is thus a matter not of rule but of regulation. Xi Kang never defines health in a canonical, theoretical mode, in comparison with ordinary health which might only seem wanting or, at best, a mere approximation of the ideal. Indeed, he is not concerned with the *state* of health, which, being fixed, is always more or less abstract, and which the Greeks conceived of in relation to the ideal constitution. What interests him instead is the *life capital* that health creates and that must be maintained and cultivated by exercising the various correlations born of its polarity (expressed as factors at once opposed and complementary, such as yin and yang).

I would therefore contrast the *correlative* logic of the Chinese with the *constitutive* logic of the Greeks, and, by the same token, I would contrast the *synthetic* harmony of the Greeks (growing out of the relationship of parts to whole) with the *regulative* harmony of the Chinese (allowing for the process to continue without end). Because the Chinese approached the real not in terms of "being" but of invested "capacity" (*de*), reserves (of immanence: the *dao*), or resources, and because, having little interest in finality, they concentrated instead on functionality (the *yong*:[d] the discreet, continuous progression of things, not the great "why" of the world), they saw "life" itself exclusively in terms of *vitality*. Thus the same Chinese verb, *sheng*,[e] means "to live," "to be born," and "to engender." The verb for "to live" remains attached to these two genetic verbs, so that "living" is not separated from the process by which it comes to pass: it does not lead into "existence" (according to the first etymological dictionary, the term *sheng* means to advance, to progress, in the sense in which vegetation grows by emerging from the earth and pushing upward). Accordingly, life potential is to be cultivated not by establishing a model for it (to be approached as a goal) but like a field (agriculture being the fundamental motif of all knowledge in this land of farmers). Knowledge of how it can be exploited and improved should be used to make it *yield* (or bear fruit) without exhausting its potential.

What is specific to "vital nourishment" is that it calls to mind both the promotion and the prolongation of life. Since health and longevity cannot be dissociated, there is no reason to choose between them. This is precisely what Francis Bacon warned against at the dawn of modern Western thought, for he held this to be impossible and therefore believed that different levels had to be distinguished: "We warn men to distinguish clearly between that which can make life healthy and that which can make it long, and carefully to separate the two."[7] On the one hand, that which serves to augment the activity of the mind and the vigor of the functions and to ward off disease "constantly detracts from the total span of life and accelerates the atrophy that constitutes aging." Conversely, that which prolongs life and wards off the atrophy of old age cannot help endangering health. The West based its heroic construction of human existence on this inexorable and tragic conflict between a full and a long life (by living life to the full, I consume myself). This tension between intensity and duration led to a privileging of health as an ideal state to the detriment of its prolongation, which could not be modeled. Thus the prolongation of life, "undeniably the most noble part of medicine," according to Bacon, is nevertheless "an entirely new part, and one that we lack completely."[8] It was at this point that a new understanding of medicine arose, one that was not merely negative or curative but that at last discovered its true object. it finally became a form of knowledge that was not hopelessly speculative. It could instead aspire to become powerfully effective, even decisive in its application, so that, by exerting influence over the essential, it could begin to revolutionize the human condition. Renaissance man, triumphant, discovered new powers due to the advancement of science and began to aspire to a mastery over nature so complete as to counter its strength and even force it into "retreat" (from old age to youth, "*remorari et retrovertere*," as Bacon puts it).[9] Having made up his mind to appropriate his life as his own property, indeed his only property, man began to reclaim it from alienating grand narratives and to trust in his new knowledge to preserve it artificially: true Christians "may long in vain for the Promised Land and hold this world to be a wasteland," yet still in their wanderings in the desert they "would rather see their habit and sandals less used" ("I mean the body," Bacon adds in clarification, "which is like the habit and sandals of the soul").[10]

Beneath the tired metaphor, ambition is conscious of its novelty. What has never been done (to prolong life) "cannot be done other than in ways that have never been attempted." But could this new knowledge, which rested on causality and served at the time in the construction of mechanistic physics, be applied to "augmenting" life as felicitously as it had been to "advancing knowledge"? In *History of Life and Death*, Bacon alternates between, on the one hand, prudent warnings and dietetic recommendations based on common sense and, on the other hand, the construction of knowledge "deduced by a very methodical procedure" but "not yet verified by experience." In linking rationality to experimentation by way of "method," Western science found a way to expand its dominion prodigiously, but when it came to knowledge not of the body but of life, the enterprise barely got off the ground. Although Descartes, too, concluded his *Discourse on Method* by raising the possibility of "exempting" ourselves from the "weakening of old age" by discovering its causes, we know that he gradually gave up the ambition of prolonging human life beyond its current limits as his research progressed.[11] Moreover, he would come to derive greater satisfaction from morality than from medicine because the former had taught him not to fear death while the latter had failed to reveal a way to preserve life.

As hopes all too hastily raised ultimately collapsed, a rupture developed in the classical period between morality and medicine, in which hygiene figured centrally. Shun all those who recommend frequent recourse to remedies, the article on hygiene in Diderot's *Encyclopédie* advises, after vaunting the merits of tranquillity and gaiety for the preservation of health. For additional evidence, we may turn to *The Conflict of the Faculties*, Kant's last published text.[12] It is oddly radical in its content and was conceived as a response to Hufeland's *Art of Prolonging Life*. It defends dietetics as a personal regimen while attacking the regulations and statutes of the faculty. Stranger still, Kant ultimately incorporated this into a logic of *conflict*, in which he made it clear that he defended the autonomy of reason and the will against the medical institution with respect to health, just as he had previously defended it against religious authority (in connection with the salvation of the soul and against the tyranny of a literal reading of the Bible) and, later, against legal authority (in connection with the social good and in regard to the codification of positive law). Kant's earliest commentators were clearly embarrassed by this and read the text, which had been conceived in terms of "exempting" oneself from old age, as a first sign of senility. Or, they simply tolerated it for its biographical interest, as Kant supposedly revealed something about his life and shared intimate details of his existence in it. Kant was supposed to have written, after his own fashion, the kind of "personal confession" that Nietzsche believed existed in all great philosophy.

When I reread this text from the perspective of "feeding life," however, I find it remarkable for quite a different reason: it shows, in the work of a philosopher reputed to be among the most abstract, the existence of a *possible alternative path* in thought. At the end of his life, Kant took a different fork, which led him some way down the very path that Chinese thought had blazed before him. Indeed, the aging Kant contemplates the gradual "extinction" of "vital force" (*Lebenskraft*) through lack of exercise. He worries about countering its "slowing" and exhaustion through "stimulation" (*Erregungsart*), imagines halting "waste" by "retrieving" what has been lost, and envisions how calculating "his quantity of life" should affect his behavior. Thus he reflects on the proper measures of sleep and nourishment and describes what breathing techniques are most suitable. He ponders the salutary functions of relaxation and of strolling so as to vary the objects that meet the eye. Indeed, he even raises a question already posed by Zhuangzi: Why does the work of philosophizing, which involves relating representations devoid of sensory intuition, lead to a loss of vitality? He abandons the "we" of ethical neutrality in order to present, as Montaigne did, an observant "I" of individual experience that communicates indirectly because it must inquire of others, as well as reveal to them, the most appropriate procedures for managing a capital that is in each case unique: as each individual ages, he or she must seek out the best path to preserve whatever vital resources and energy remain. For instance, Kant describes the tactic he has worked out and the indifferent object (Cicero) on which he fixes his attention in the evening so that he can fall asleep.

But what overall conception comparable to Xi Kang's can Kant rely on to demonstrate the soundness of this approach to personal hygiene, as opposed to the heteronomy of medical remedies and prescriptions? The principle he invokes, which is moral in essence, is one of pure and simple "resolution" (*blosser und fester Vorsatz*), stoic in character, and consciously opposed to "facility" (*Gemächlichkeit*: the facility of eating [too much] or sleeping [too much] or being lazy, and so on). The power of a *dietetics of thought* is such that it can teach us to amuse ourselves by practicing alternation (the philosopher deciding to stop thinking temporarily) so as to relax the mind. If I wish to rest, it is enough that I *will* a halt to my thinking. How can one help noticing, however, how inadequate this self-determination of the will, which dominates in the ethical domain, turns out to be when it comes to managing our *health-capital*, and how easily it can be turned against it? Thus Kant, too, concludes with renunciation: the "art of prolonging life" can only lead, especially in the case of a philosopher, to the "invalidism" of a depleted life, whereupon it can only be "tolerated" miserably.

Comparison with the Daoist man of letters will thus give us a better idea of what in China created a middle level between medicine and morality (or "body" and "soul") and thus encouraged hygienic thought. It will also help us imagine conditions under which the possibility of further theoretical development might arise today. For instance, the idea of alternation — between activity and rest, "gripping" and "releasing," tension and relaxation — may not need to come under the head of a stoic decision, as it does in Kant. Instead, it can be included from the outset within the overarching logic of regulation, in which each member of a pair brings on and continues the other — a logic that Chinese thinkers always sought to elucidate. In the most general sense, with regard to both heaven and man, the Chinese tradition thought primarily in terms of "nonexhaustion"[f] through "constant modification" ("modification" being that which permits "continuation": *bian-tong*)[g] Similarly, the importance attached to respiration in China can be incorporated into the more common idea that, so long as change continues, life is maintained by the removal of obstructions and by "communication" (*tong*).

In explaining the Chinese predisposition to think in terms of hygiene, I shall limit myself to three points. First, if nourishment not only serves to feed the "body" (materially) but also directly stimulates or calms both my energetic capacity and spirit (which are, in any case, inseparable), it is because all nourishment is, as we have seen, the *concentration of breath-energy*. Xi Kang, in referring to the very detailed knowledge embodied in the Chinese pharmacopoeia, cannot help noticing the enhancement of vitality and effects on longevity attributed to various plants, which are said to produce a "transformation-refinement" (*jing*:[h] the very term with which we began). Second, what distinguishes hygienic thought from our "physical" knowledge, including medicine, is that it is based on an idea not of causality but of *influence* (influence of food, activity, climate, season, and so on). Not being a thought centered around essence or "quiddity" (which invites the introduction of a causal relationship), Chinese thought was conceived in terms of exhalation-impregnation, or incitation and reaction. Effects, no matter how remote, could remain correlated for indefinite periods (which accounts for the importance accorded to notions of atmosphere, milieu, and ambience, even in the political realm). Xi Kang compiled lists of such effects, ranging from the most palpable, which no one would contest, to the more subtle, which are no less important. Third, ultimately, hygiene can be conceived only in relation to the *subtle* as it gradually spreads and unfolds over the course of time. A factor or phenomenon that at first passed unnoticed may nevertheless be ripe with consequences later on, solely because of the process it initiates. The logic of hygiene is one of *propensity*. The Chinese mind, whether engaged in thoughts of hygiene, morality, or strategy, is always prepared to scrutinize the *infinitesimal*,[i] the source of evolutions whose ultimate consequence, unfolding of its own accord, is *infinite*. By the same token, Xi Kang observes, if a single watering can delay a drought, a single rage may attack our nature and initiate its corruption. If we ordinarily disdain the hygiene of vital nourishment, it is because we do not know how to perceive the subterranean maturation of its effect. We wait, then, until the result is manifest, apparently emerging out of nowhere (as when we "fall" ill), before we apply the remedy. We wait until we experience symptoms, in other words, before we begin treatment. By contrast, since Chinese thought approaches the real in terms of reserves (of capacity) and the associated processes, it invites us to attend to the slightest deviation well in advance of the crisis that will some day result from it. If we do that, Xi Kang tells us, we realize that the crisis has no "beginning"; we are surprised by the suddenness of an event only when we fail to perceive the silent transformation by which the malady has logically progressed.

Bacon boldly hoped that science might prolong life by thwarting nature and forcing it to retreat. Kant, renouncing this ambition, trusted in the only power otherwise left to us: resolution of the will. By contrast, the Daoist man of letters proposes to prolong life by wedding the processive logic of transformation through refinement-decantation to that of influence and reactivity, which is visible everywhere in nature. That is why, in Xi Kang, prolonging life can describe life's very horizon and take the place of both morality and religion. Going back to "fundamentals," he retreats into the desperate desire to endure. Yet if I make staying alive my life's central concern, I encounter a conflict of values that obliges me to justify myself. Not that I project staying alive as a "goal," of course. Nor do I revert to the elementary desire and instinct of self-preservation (Xi Kang's text is free of any kind of psychological justification, and this, for me, is its greatest merit). So I must justify myself, even if I had fervently hoped to escape the ideological by confining myself to the terrain of the vital, where all must tread and which remains, no matter what one does, the most basic. For I run up against the question of the legitimacy of what nevertheless remains a choice.[13] And if I radicalize my position, I run up against the barricade of disbelief: Xi Kang met with the skepticism of those who were suspicious of long life, just as religion in Europe is vulnerable to the skepticism of those who do not believe in eternal life.

Accordingly, he was obliged, at the end of his essay, to refute them. If one is preoccupied with the realm of ordinary people, he argues, one sees a limited life span everywhere and therefore believes that this is the common law. Those who hear of ways of "feeding life" nevertheless cling to what they have seen and decide that such a thing is impossible. Others may raise questions, but if they approach the path, they do not know how to start down it. Still others will assiduously consume drugs for six months or a year, but, when they see no result, their will flags, and they stop mid course. Yet others may economize on little things and indulge themselves in big ones, while waiting, "seated" (that is, passively), for the result to come about by itself. Others may repress their emotions and renounce their appetite for glory, but with the object of their desire before them and the object of their hopes still dozens of years in the future, they fear losing both. They begin to doubt and struggle with themselves until, caught between the near (which attracts them) and the far (of promise), they get exhausted and give up. Since none of these people understand that everything is decided at a more subtle stage — which only the "reason of things" allows one to discern initially and which, for a long time, remains difficult to appreciate in a tangible way — they fail to persevere long enough to see the result appear. With an "impatient spirit," they see a path of evanescence, discretion, and "placidity." They want to move quickly, but the situation evolves slowly. They hope for a short-term benefit, whereas the "answer" is remote. Failure is inevitable. They lack the knowledge necessary to overcome the hasty perspective of their emotional excitement and to take the longer view appropriate to the way phenomena evolve and mature. They fail to understand that one cannot will, much less precipitate, access to serenity, on which health and longevity nevertheless ultimately depend.

CHAPTER ELEVEN

Anti-Stress: Cool, Zen, and So On

Nowadays, a new notion seems to have subsumed the pressures from the world and from within ourselves that turn into inner tension. "Stress," with its intense and prolonged sibilant, in some ways evokes the meaning of the Latin *stringere*: to squeeze, compress, strangle. It expresses the degree to which "pressure" finds its way inside us. Straddling any number of fields carefully separated by disciplinary boundaries (psychology, physiology, neurochemistry, sociology, and so on) and silently spreading its tentacles to undermine those disciplines' justifications and divisions, the notion has grown uncontrollably for decades. It now refers to that which is disturbed and disrupted by excess *stimulation* to the point of paralyzing our vitality. The model, the initial image, is, of course, the metal bar that bends and is deformed when a weight is placed on it. "That which is disturbed": classical science is disappointed — defeated? — by the fact that for once it cannot locate whatever it is more precisely than this. That is why this notion, brought to our attention or, rather, imposed by common usage, poses a major challenge to our theoretical ambition. This is so not only because it breaks down disciplinary boundaries and reveals the degree to which the separation of the psychic and the somatic is even less tenable than we had previously believed, but especially because all knowledge is, in itself, specific, while this notion forces us to de-specify. In contrast to medical science, which progressed steadily by studying ever more closely the *sui generis* reaction of the organism to disease, the study of stress obliges us to recognize that a syndrome has a generalized status that, in principle, baffles any attempt to break it down or classify it. Over the centuries, Western thinkers have learned to distinguish objects with ever greater precision and have broken human experience into separate compartments, in particular the medical, moral, and spiritual. "Stress," however, is like a password, or rather an impasse-word, that allows the repressed to return again and again. "I'm stressed out" is the antonym of the discreet "I'm fine," and nowadays it is just as commonplace. What began as a technical term in physics was peremptorily taken up by everyday thought and has become a symptomatic cliché. It is almost an admonition that reminds us to pay attention not so much to classical notions, such as the "unity" or globality of the living, but rather to *indivisibility*. In this respect, the word points to the same thing as the concept of "feeding life," but it does so from the opposite direction.

Similar attention should be paid to the opposites of "stress," the words we invoke to free ourselves from its grip. These, too, filter up from below, if I may put it that way, without reference to established knowledge, and maintain themselves through fashion and repetition (in everyday language, subway signs, advertising, and so on): I am thinking of the words *cool*, *zen*, and the like — ingenuous, tenuous, atheoretical words. It is as if there were no choice but to resort to these words without status or even content, if we want to call for the immediate removal of obstacles and fixations and a return to the fluidity of life. Why must we resort to such terms to express the liberation from stress, itself a word borrowed from elsewhere? What is being sought with such words that cannot otherwise be expressed? This is tantamount to

asking how the standard discourse of the disciplines must be broken down if we are to begin to make surreptitious headway. Might
it simply be that the effect of using foreign terminology is para-
doxical? It *dilutes* meaning as well as *promotes* it, helping to get
across what would otherwise be expressed reductively in notions
that are too specific for the purpose and lack stimulative force —
insipid, abstract, and consequently sterile notions (such as "relax-
ing," "chilling out," and "hanging loose," which are too physical,
and blessed "serenity," which is too idyllic)? The semantic ambiguity of these terms would then count as a plus, facilitating the
loosening or relaxation of our grip, and so would its evocative
power, which the metaphorical transference into a different
idiom encourages, at once heightening the meaning and setting
it off.

Or might it be, more gravely, that in order to react to stress
and free ourselves from it, we must look for support not traditionally provided by our education, returning to what constitutes
us anthropologically? In any case, "cool" and "zen" discreetly
take us outside the realms of morality and psychology, the two
established pillars of behavior in the West. "Be cool" might suggest a retreat to a level less subject to voluntary choice, one involving a certain degree of "temperament." The allusion would
be to something akin to the traditional, if largely imaginary, codification of the *ethos* of various peoples, as when we refer to the
"phlegmatic temperament" of the British. Or perhaps this is
already too elaborate a construct and the phrase instead conveys
images of a more relaxed way of life that has resulted from changes
in our material civilization (and its forced Americanization, with
Coke, jeans, T-shirts, sneakers, and all the rest), a way of life that
is perhaps mainly the province of youth. Are we talking about a
cultural revolution or an erosion of "standards" and "values"? If
the latter, there would scarcely be any reason for us to abandon

or invert our usual categories or question our theoretical choices.

"Be *zen*," on the other hand, might get us out of this dilemma, for in a discreet but decisive way this injunction may open up a novel avenue of communication between spirituality and the flourishing of vitality. The spirituality at issue here is not the constructed, theological kind that has us *seeking* God or some monopoly of divine love in a tense quest. Rather, it calls for the release of tension: inner detachment and emptiness, like that which appeared in the *Zhuangzi* (bear in mind that *zen* is the Chinese appropriation and radicalization of Buddhism), are paramount. Dogmatic obstacles vanish, along with all notional content, and even the imperious insistence on truth. Yet this is not relativism or skepticism stemming from the "abandonment" of truth, even if relativism and skepticism are obligatory stages in arriving at this destination (this is, in fact, the subject of *Zhuangzi*'s second chapter, the most theoretical of all, whose title hints at its significance: "On the Equality of Things and Discourses"). Indeed, the "plenitude" that Zhuangzi calls on us to relinquish involves not appearances but impediments: to denounce it is not to denounce a metaphysical illusion but to give up the way our attachment to things impedes the spontaneous development of processes. Similarly, the "void" that Zhuangzi urges us to recover is less inherent than immanent: it is not the manifestation of some (ontological) "nothingness" but the vehicle through which enough space and emptiness are created for effects to unfold. Life can escape whatever confines it and regain its freedom, allowing it to remain open to unfettered transformation. Based on deliberate de-ontologization (and de-theologization), this *release* from meaning (from dogma, belief, truth) results in a depressurization of existence, which ceases to be episodic or forced. The homeostasis whereby *life* maintains itself is restored, replacing the tension of *existence* (projecting toward a goal, akin to meaning).

"Be *zen*": as commonplace as the expression has become, it remains an absurdity, a contradiction in terms, *contradictio in adjecto*. Access to *zen* cannot be the object of any command; it resists the imperative mode. Indeed, it is not until we have freed ourselves from every "thou shalt" and, above all, from the commandment to free ourselves, that access to *zen* is achieved (and we realize what *zen* is). Trust in immanence (that which "comes thus of its own accord," *ziran*) cannot be *commanded*. It is here, it seems to me, that Western Stoicism, which made such heavy use of the imperative, meets its ethical limit. The "systematic" (if ever anything was) connection that Stoicism established between its ethics and its "physics" turns out to be weak. Even if its physics is no longer riveted to being, it is still too encumbered by its insistence on living "in conformity with nature" to indulge of its own accord in rest. *Zen* can be achieved, by contrast, only by abandoning the quest and the goal, which is what it takes disciples so long to grasp as they proceed from temple to temple. Not that it is necessary, in the end, to renounce the "tending toward" (the *ephiesthai* of the Greeks on which I commented earlier); nor are we limited to discovering a goal immanent in the act itself or in the event (the "autotelism" of the Stoics). Without any object of striving, this vacuity is suddenly transformed into plenitude (or the "transparency of morning," as Zhuangzi puts it, after describing the "whole world" and "things" and even concern for one's own "life" as "external" elements that no longer encumber one's vitality). Or, rather, even this opposition disappears: such "transparency" is achieved precisely when these factitious disjunctions (plenitude versus vacuity, and so on) cease to interpose themselves as screens. If we remain open to both fullness and emptiness and refuse to assign an end stage *unfettered evolution* then becomes possible. As Zhuangzi's text proceeds, it moves along the path where the "rested" and "relaxed" being (*xiaoran*)[a]

141

understands itself logically, dissolving the tension that stems as much from disjunctive oppositions as from the fixation on a goal. The two inevitably go together: the "way" on which we forever "allow things to happen" goes with the one which we "accompany without inquiry," and the "way" on which we neither "forget the beginning nor seek to know the ultimate end"[1] coincides with the one which creates a way out distinct from a form of happiness predicated on finality.

By contrast, it is the sovereign force of resolution, supported by the progressive constitution of the apparatus of will that dominated the classical age, that seems to me to have blocked the way to a concept of *anti-stress* in the West. This leads Westerners today to use frivolous and quirky terms such as "cool," "zen," and the like, in order to make way for the *relaxation* whose salutary effects invariably elicit comment. Note that Galen developed his materialist theory of the soul sufficiently to remark that "the faculties of the soul follow the temperaments of the body."[2] Note also that, if nourishment and, more broadly, diet determine the temperaments of the body, it should be possible to influence the faculties of the soul directly: clearly, it was assumed that the psychic could depend on material factors. Conversely, medical science did not shrink away from explaining in causal terms how negative psychological events could affect health adversely. Witness Descartes: "The most common cause of slow fever," he remarked to Princess Elizabeth, "is melancholy."[3] If the mind is affected, the circulation of the blood can be slowed, so that the cruder parts coagulate, "obstructing the spleen," while the more subtle parts affect the lungs and provoke coughing. Only by imposing an inner discipline in a strictly Stoic manner — withdrawing both the imagination and the senses from unhappy events so that they no longer make an impression, and seeking our contentment in overcoming trials and tribulations — can we remedy such physical decline.

Western philosophers not only insisted on this, but they first and foremost insisted on it for themselves. Kant was pleased he was able to overcome the tendency toward hypochondria that resulted from the smallness of his chest by imposing a spiritual diet on himself. Descartes believed that his penchant, born of determination, for looking at things "from the angle that made them most agreeable to me" enabled him to overcome the cough and pallor he had inherited from his mother, which all the doctors agreed doomed him to an early end. The philosopher thus counted on his Stoic will and determination to establish a discipline that would save him from his own fragility. Hence he only glimpsed in passing what a de-stressing relaxation might look like and was unable to explore the matter further. When Descartes lectures a young woman about how the waters of Spa can be good for the circulation, he mentions the physicians' recommendation to "do nothing but imitate those who contemplate the green of the forest, the color of a flower, the flight of a bird, and other things that require no attention and thus persuade themselves that they have emptied their minds of thought." To behave in this way, Descartes insists, "is not to waste time but to use it well, for we can take satisfaction from the hope that in this way we can regain our perfect health, which is the most fundamental of all the goods we can have in this life."[4] He says nothing more — indeed, he *cannot* say anything more. What he does say, moreover, is said only in passing. To empty the mind of thought: What is the meaning of this "empty"? Does it not contradict the very possibility of thought in this metaphysical thinker? If "thinking of nothing" is for Descartes an extreme case that signals the end of reflection, beyond which he cannot go, it is of course because no intuition of a more radical emptiness is available to him. Because he cannot make the connection with the true de-ontologization (the beneficial detachment and release) that his own experience has revealed, he falls back on the Stoic advice that he lacks the means to transcend.

In his chapter "The World of Human Affairs," Zhuangzi recounts the following stressful situation as a typical case, and it leads him to clarify the nature of the "nourishment" that can remedy it.

> Just before leaving on a mission to Qi, Zigao, the duke of Ye, consulted Confucius.
>
> "The king has entrusted me with a very important mission. Of course you know that Qi treats ambassadors with ostentatious respect, but he is in no haste [to accede to their requests]. It is difficult to influence even an ordinary man, much less a prince. I am very worried about it.
>
> You often say, 'In all affairs, large or small, there are few in which we are not eager for success. If we do not succeed, men treat us ill. If we do succeed, we invariably suffer from an imbalance of yin and yang. To avoid the unfortunate consequences of success and failure — only a man gifted with abundant capacity can do that.'
>
> The meals in my home are frugal and plain. No one in my kitchens needs to seek out a cool place. Yet this morning I received my orders, and tonight I am reduced to drinking ice water. My mission has made me hot. I have not yet even embarked on the business, and already I am suffering from disturbances of the yin and the yang."[5]

There is nothing ambiguous about the case in point: the disturbance of the yin and the yang is clearly a physiological disequilibrium brought about by the stress of the mission. Stimulation has produced an inner warming that has not yet risen to the level

of a fever but already indicates a generalized disorder, the nonspe-
cific response of the organism to the stressing agent (stressor).
Confucius (to whom Zhuangzi attributes his response) initially
answers with a conventional lesson, stoic in its tenor: "Under
heaven there are two great commandments: one is fate, the other
duty." To love one's parents is "fate" and "cannot be banished
from one's heart." To serve one's prince is "duty," which is incum-
bent on the subject everywhere, and "no one in this world can
escape such obligations." It follows that the subject must forget
his own wishes and deal with the situation as best he can. What
leisure would there be "in loving life and hating death"? There is
no choice but to submit to duty, to confront fate.

This, in words that Zhuangzi attributes to Confucius, is the
easy, conventional lesson, which affords comfort through inner
resolve and acceptance of the inevitable. But the passage continues in a different tone, revealing a different possibility that subtly
circumvents this advice: "By relying on external things so as to
allow your spirit to evolve freely, you trust in what cannot be otherwise in such a way as to nourish your inner equilibrium."

Here the disciple is discreetly invited to distance himself from
the stoic order, to make use of the outside world and its diversity
— to "mount" the world and sit astride it, the text says — so as to
maintain the freedom of his innermost self. Instead of holding
firmly to some fixed position or feeling, the disciple is urged to
continue to "evolve" in an unpressured, relaxed, comfortable,
unfettered way (you,[b] which is Zhuangzi's master-word for the
dissipation of stress). Rather than allow himself to be carried
away by the *stimulation* of the temporarily imposed mission, he is
to "trust" in the *incitement* that comes to us most intrinsically
from the world and "cannot be otherwise." "Feeding" one's inner
equilibrium (*yang zhong*),[c] then, corresponds exactly, I believe, to
the notion of homeostasis that I proposed earlier, which has been

used by theorists of stress to support the idea of a basic regulation of the individual that is at once psychic, emotional, and somatic. Ultimately, this is what we "nourish" most fundamentally when we cease to talk about nourishing either the soul or the body, when that alternative is at last transcended, leaving only vital potential in its indivisible unity. We nourish equilibrium (the "center," the "median") by harmonizing yin and yang so as to alleviate the pressure on both: yin anxiety before the mission is completed, as well as yang contentment when it has been successfully concluded. Thus, in our harmoniously *evolving perseverance*, we cannot distinguish among the demands of the vital, the moral, and the spiritual (or even the cosmic).

I see yet another reason to dwell on the short, discreet, light-hearted terms *cool* and *zen*, beyond the benefit derived from their strangeness and even from the incidental way they displace the moral and psychological landmarks we use to guide and judge our behavior. This has to do with the poetics of the words themselves. When I say *cool*, it is easy to see that what counts is not so much the "intrinsic" meaning of the word as the nonchalant *oo* sound, which laps the lips as a wave laps the shore, quelling and dissipating tension as it ebbs. The word itself mimics the gradual process of discharging and silencing a stimulus until it is fully absorbed. *Zen* is barely even a word, but it has a certain resonance, akin to that of the string of a bow between the fingers after the arrow has been fired. The original Chinese word, *chan* (pronounced *tchan*), does not have the same effect: *zen* is more vibrant, less expansive. It merely points, without encumbering itself with meaning or erecting itself into a notion. Both words obviously benefit from being monosyllabic (relaxation, release, repose, and serenity are too complex). Now, Zhuangzi deliberately sought such effects as well. Of the sovereign of the great extremity it is said: "He slept

xu-xu [pronounced *shu-shu*], awoke *yu-yu*."[6] Although the commentary glosses the first term as "relaxed, in comfort" and the
second as "content with himself" (which Liu translates as "sleeps
peacefully" and "wakes up relaxed" and Graham translates as
"slept soundly and woke up fresh"), what matters most here is the
impression made by the two words (reinforced by repetition),
since the second has almost no specific meaning.[7] The term not
only de-specifies but also de-signifies. By insisting on such a relaxation of meaning, the text liberates the spirit from the pressure
in which belonging to the human race immerses us. This pressure
is our most constant source of stress — barely alleviated even by
sleep — the pressure exerted by the codifications and directions of
language.

Zhuangzi expresses this de-stressing relaxation (of meanings,
actions, and obligations) in a number of ways, surreptitiously
nudging us away from voluntary resolution. Yet everything starts
with something like a Stoic *topos*: the vicissitudes of life and death,
survival and loss, misery and glory, poverty and wealth, and so
on, "are not important enough to disturb our personal harmony
or to penetrate to our innermost selves."[8] But the difference from
Stoicism again lurks in the background. "Wisdom," we are told,
consists in seeing to it that we can "continue" and "move beyond"
these vicissitudes (by remaining in "communication" with ourselves and with the world, according to the double meaning of
tong),[d] making it so they can never stand as obstructions (and,
thus, so we never relinquish our "bliss"). Once again, the Daoist
sage puts words in Confucius's mouth: it is enough if, "day and
night, without the slightest interruption, we remain as fresh as
springtime in our relations with the world." As in Chinese martial
arts, the absence of any interruption in the dynamic flow indicates one must remain open to the virtue of transition *per se*; similarly, the invocation of springtime does not instruct us to remain

attached to spring (and therefore regret its passing) but tells us to keep pace with life's constant growth. Such persistence, unlike Stoicism, is *evolving*, not *resolute*. It is not simply a matter of maintaining a harmonious and positive relation to the world, as Chinese commentators initially understood it. It is also "to evolve in concert with the world," as the seasons do, so that through all its vicissitudes (and owing to the very constancy of change) we maintain our vitality as fresh as it was in its inception — *springtime*.

This liberating relaxation stands in sharp contrast to both self-indulgent indifference and willful rigidity. It transcends parasitic stimuli and excitations to remain open to the constant flux of incentives that replenishes the world. It requires physical conditioning and *upkeep*. It obliges us to modify our behavior, or, rather, it results from such a modification. Indeed, this is something that most clearly distinguishes the teaching of vital nourishment from philosophy. When Chipped Tooth asks the Clothed One about the "way," *dao*, in the *Zhuangzi*, the latter responds: "Straighten up your body, unify your vision, and the [natural] harmony of Heaven will come to you. Curb your intelligence, unify your attitude, and the [dimension of] spirit will come to dwell in you."[9] When "the way dwells in you, your pupils will be like those of a newborn," your gaze will be naive, ingenuous, uninformed, and "you will no longer ask questions about causality." The sempiternal and exhausting *why* of things will at last come up empty. In zen temples, of course, one of the first lessons taught is how to sit up straight but without rigidity, in a "correct" but unforced posture: neither rigid nor slumped. Unless one masters this, there is no point in staying. More than any words, this silent correctness of posture in itself leads to a proper attitude. It is enough to sit properly on the harsh ground so that the "dorsal artery" (*du*: through which the energetic circulation flows) is in the proper position. There should be no effort to hold oneself erect or strive for any goal. Inner obstructions and coagulations will then dissolve. Such a "unification of attitude" restores communication between inside and outside, so that the world is once again "lodged" in the world, and beings "dwell in their uses," as Zhuangzi says. The stressful urge to impart meaning (to life, death, and so on) dissipates. Zen refers to the consistent achievement of such an effect, which is as much a sensation as an idea, as well as the unambiguous foundation of zen teaching. Relaxation is so fully achieved in this passage that Chipped Tooth, at last relinquishing the tedious inquiries of intelligence, "falls into a deep sleep" even before the Clothed One has finished speaking. The humor is directed at both the prescriptions of ritual and the relationship between master and disciple, which one must learn to reverse.

Chapter Twelve

Condemned to the Eternal Silence

of Processes

After considering and refuting the various reasons why so many people are unnecessarily suspicious of the long life, Xi Kang ends his essay "on feeding life" by explicitly associating the theme of vital nourishment, inherited from Zhuangzi, with the anti-stress and hygiene themes of longevity. The conclusion deserves to be translated in its entirety for its assured manner: an even tension is maintained throughout, from one element to the next (there is no longer any pretense of an argument), so as to present regulation as a self-contained and smoothly coherent package. All fluctuation of tone is banished, and not so much as a whisper of emotion remains:

> But one who is skilled at nourishing life is not like this. Pure, empty, tranquil, at peace, "he diminishes self-interest and lessons his desires." He knows that fame and position injure virtue; therefore he disregards them and seeks them not. It is not that he desires them but forcefully forbids them. He knows that rich flavors harm the nature; therefore he rejects them and pays them no mind. It is not that he first longs for them and only then represses [his true feelings]. External things, because they ensnare the mind, he does not maintain. Spirit and breath, because they are unsullied and pure, on these alone

is his attention focussed. Open and unrestrained is he, free from worry and care, silent and still, devoid of thought and concern. Furthermore, he maintains this state with the one and nourishes it with harmony. Harmony and principle daily increase and he becomes one with the Great Accord [Great Natural Conformity]. After this he steams [himself] with magic fungus and soaks in sweet water from a spring; dries [himself] off in the morning sun and soothes [himself] with the five strings. Without action and self-attained, his body ethereal and mind profound, he forgets happiness, and as a result his joy is complete; he leaves life behind, and as a result his person is preserved. If he can go on from this, he can come close to comparing in old age with Hsien-men and matching his years with Prince Ch'iao. How can it be that such people do not exist?[1]

Here, the recapitulation creates a claustrophobic effect, and the text settles into self-congratulation, yielding to its various penchants and discreetly withdrawing from debate. Its art lies in the easy glide from sentence to sentence (a far remove from the polemical violence and even insistence of the Stoics). Themes previously evoked press on one another to cover the entire range of the thinkable, leaving nothing untouched. Everything comes together in this final bouquet: how to "keep" (one's) vitality by liberating and unifying it (see Chapter One); refinement of one's physical being, which becomes more "subtle," while at the same time "deepening" the spirit (see Chapter Two); reduction of one's selfish interest in order to achieve full self-possession, along with the "abandonment of one's life" in order to facilitate its unfolding (see Chapter Three); inner vacancy and idleness based on the immanence of the great natural conformity (compare the de-ontologization of Chapters Four and Eleven); purification of the breath-energy leading to unfolding of the spiritual dimension (*shen-qi*;[a] see Chapter Seven); procedures of vital nourishment that culmi-

nate in an intimate relationship of participation and accompani-
ment with the elements of the world, the sources of pure water
and the rising sun (see Chapter Eight); "bliss" as the result of
oblivion, of "forgetting" to seek contentment, as all pursuits of
happiness dissolve in plenitude ("he forgets happiness, and as a
result his joy is complete," is Robert G. Henricks's translation;[2]
see Chapter Nine); the logic of influence through impregnation-
imbibing and the notion of the inherent "coherence" (*li*)[b] of the
vital as the basis of hygiene and longevity (see Chapter Ten); and
vital nourishment, understood as "homeostasis" that encourages
"harmony" and relaxation in the face of stressful pressure (see
Chapter Eleven). Note that a notion of the soul is never mentioned in any of this, and that what we designate by the unitary
term "body" is here divided between constitutive being, on the
one hand, and personal life, on the other (recall that the compound of the two, *shen-ti*, emerges as a stable expression for body
only in modern Chinese; see Chapter Five and Six).

It is admirable how subtly all these themes are woven together. They shed light on one another without any imperious
need for a system to organize them. The vital becomes the basis
of a unitary vision, which, in effect, takes the place of morality as
well as religion. Indeed, the mesh appears to be so fine that it
excludes all ambiguity, doubt, and anxiety and leaves no opportunity for deviation — to the point that it stifles cries, laughter,
pathos, jubilation, and so on. Is this denial? It is equally surprising
to see what this epilogue resolutely omits — in particular, the
"other," in any of its many guises, is rigorously ignored. Descartes's solipsism was temporary, but the solipsism in which the
adept of long life buries himself (in his indefinite embrace of what
is implied by "harmony") is permanent. He will never encounter
anything capable of extracting him from it. Hence there is no
room for speech either — not even reflexive speech addressed to

oneself. If to think is to dialogue with oneself, does the sage think? Elucidation of the coherence inherent in the vital presumably takes place before language introduces disjunction by severing of words from things. Xi Kang's conclusion thus erases itself. It proposes no message, and no meaning can be inferred.

It would be easy to contrast this portrait of the adept of long life with the way its author died. Xi Kang was related by marriage to the recently overthrown ruling family and did everything he could throughout his life to remain aloof from politics and its torments. One day, a powerful courtier named Zhong Hui honored him with a visit, but Xi Kang continued to work metal in his forge as if his guest were not there. Melting crude matter to obtain something purer and stronger from it — was this not what he was trying to do to himself, to forge an imperishable body? And is not that which lies between "heaven and earth" all around us, like "a great bellows" maintaining cosmic energy in constant motion, according to Laozi?[3] The lesson regarding the importunate guest is clear: Xi Kang will not allow himself to be distracted by affairs of the world.

Although it is possible to remain aloof from the rivalries and vanities of politics, one cannot shun *the political* with impunity. By surrendering to the unitary celebration of "harmony" and refusing to accept dissonance with "the natural" in order to reflect on the conditions of autonomy, and, further, by failing to conceive of any essence, form, or model (of the right or the good) external to and transcending the world toward which his aspirations might "tend," the Chinese man of letters subjected himself to the arbitrary application of force, which he had no means to challenge. Legitimating that force in cosmological terms — heaven and earth, yin and yang — only increases the alienation. By refusing to conceptualize conflict, he enslaved himself. By conceiving of the ideal of "availability" as a *comprehensive* disposition of his personality, so that he was equally open to any and every possibility and did not rule anything out *a priori*, his conduct evolved solely in response to his situation. He therefore ultimately fails to develop any *position* vis-à-vis power — for a position implies an end to flow, blockage, and partiality. By refusing to take sides, "standing neither for nor against," as Confucius recommended,[4] he has made it impossible for himself to constitute *another side* (different from that of power) and closed off the possibility of dissidence. Thus the Chinese man of letters never transformed himself into an intellectual, backed by an order of values other than that derived from history. For a — liberating — order of the political to have been constituted and institutionalized, an ideal would have had to be designated, an ideal distinct from the functionality of process, which Chinese thought conceptualized as permanently harmonious. In other words, a *utopia* would have to have been produced. In Greece, the concept of utopia goes back at least to Plato's *Republic*. This was the purpose of the West's tenacious devotion to the idea of happiness. This idea of happiness, constantly in need of renovation, was the price — the heavy price — that had to be paid in order for the political to emerge as a *separate* order, favorable to autonomy.

Lacking this, the Chinese man of letters found himself without resources. Throughout nearly two millennia of history, his only options were to serve the prince or to fall back on personal development. He established no rights of any kind: no right of self-defense or contradiction, much less of criticism. Although a duty of "remonstrance" was ascribed to him vis-à-vis the prince (at his own risk, to be sure), protest as such was forbidden. *In the name of what* could he protest? Xi Kang's biography is a case in point. Because of his association with a nasty family dispute, in which he played no part, it was easy for the powers of the day to charge him with a crime and send him to prison. Any pretext was good enough to get rid of a man who not only refused a career but also implied by his actions that there really was no need for the state apparatus that was supposed to maintain the great natural regulation at the human level. The state inevitably intervened between personal development cultivated in the name of long life and the cosmic order its adepts invoked. Thus the alternative — reimagined in literary tradition as harmonious "alternation" between "advance" and "retreat," between service and retirement, between courtly duties and the solitude of bamboo, fingering the lute — was of course fundamentally only an illusion (a mere escape, *without utopian overtones*) ill concealed by endless repetition. The outcome was hardly in doubt.

Xi Kang was condemned to death at the age of thirty-nine. The three thousand students of the great school petitioned that he be made their master. This was the only attempt to save him, and the request was not granted. Worse than the injustice of his death was the fact that it served no purpose. Unlike Socrates's death, which set an example and embodied an ideal signifying another order of values, Xi Kang's death — though widely mourned and cited so frequently that it became a literary *topos* — never served to justify revolt or sustain hope or thought of progress. And for good reason: there was no trial, no argument for or against, no clash of views (for want of an appropriate institution); there was nothing like the Greek "antilogy." The *unspoken*, the power of allusion, prevailed, and this sapped the power to construct a *position* by refutation. Only by default does Xi Kang embody nonconformism and the perils it entails (which are worth meditating on). Even worse, his last poem, "Obscure Sadness," written in prison, though widely read and included in numerous anthologies, was glossed as the ultimate sign of humility, in which the author supposedly expressed his repentance to the powers that be. There was no escape from the ideological framework of the great and supposedly natural functionality — it closed over him and swallowed him up. Power inevitably had the last word, since no rival discourse emerged. When the time set for his execution arrived, Xi Kang allegedly played "Ode to the Great Peace" on his lute one last time. What choice did he have other than to invoke harmony *yet again*? Then, as he was being put to death, he reportedly turned to face his shadow. Alas, it was still there, following him as always. The Daoists believed that a person who had refined and decanted his nature to the point that he no longer cast a shadow could rest assured that his material nature had been purified and become imperishable.

Having explored Xi Kang's fate, we are in a position to understand that he not only lacked an Other and a language but that he also sought to protect himself from any relation to temporality. Can he therefore truly be called a "subject"? Even though he does not mystically identify with the All (or divinity) but simply "attains" or "obtains" himself[c] by refraining from action and, indeed, abandoning his life, he is said to be in a position to "ensure the existence of his own person."[d] Even if what is at stake is his individual life (and what is more strictly individual than one's life capital?), he is nevertheless devoid of all personality and character in the end. Nothing seems to leave a trace in him. There is no focal point, no grain of solidity in all this fluidity. Having freed himself from any possibility of being trapped, he has also placed himself beyond the reach of any event, be it traumatic or ecstatic. Avoiding love or hate, he lacks any "object," so that, strictly speaking, nothing can happen to him. Thus free of personal history, he becomes all the more vulnerable to that great consumer of energy, history writ large.

Consequently, this figure of wisdom is of more than just ideological interest. Psychoanalysis may also find this case worthwhile to ponder, if only because it seems so foreign to the psychoanalytic approach that it may hint at an alternative. A comparison might suggest alternative modes of self-transformation: metapsychological investigation and deciphering of the repressed in psychoanalysis vs. refinement and freeing of one's energy in vital nourishment. The two run parallel to one another, each insisting, perhaps, on the exclusion of the other. Might nourishment be the "other solution"? Rather than investigate our past relationship to the other (through the talking cure, transference, and so on) in the hope of exploring an unconscious existential intricacy that is the source of both neurosis and personality (sexual as well as experiential), we might seek a very different kind of liberation. It would be a transformation of our "ways" of communication, both internal and with the "world," physical and physiological as well as psychic, so as to ensure that our constitutive being (not just our "soul" or "body") "keeps" evolving. One would then rely not on introspection but on the elementary faculty of respiration (and thus on the "internal gaze" directed toward one's energies, calm, proper position, and so on). One would count not on the power of determination and liberation through speech (although psychoanalysts are, of course, wary of the function of confession) but on a capacity for "voiding" and "evacuation" through procedures of detachment and concentration that would reestablish complete processivity throughout one's being and restore the unity of the organic and the mental. This continues until the "transparency of morning" is attained, at which point life is cleansed of its opacity and everything is once again part of a process of development. "Meditation," the term most commonly used in the West today to designate this activity of internal harmonization, turns out to be inadequate for expressing this process of "nourishment" and *integralization* that develops vitality to the full.

In any case, what is important is not that these two possibilities exist side by side, so that people today can participate *either* in the great Western tradition of *catharsis* — aimed at purging and transforming emotions, and from which psychoanalysis ultimately derives — *or* in the great Chinese tradition of the *dao* and cosmic-energetic regulation. So what if one knocks at the door of the Eastern master practicing the art of long life or the Western analyst practicing the art of the couch (just as there are two medicines, two cuisines, and so on)? What matters more, I think, is that the parallel existence of these two practices points toward a common *de-finalization* of existence based solely on managing the way we care for ourselves. Both practices aim to reduce obstructions and blockages by freeing us from adherences and fixations and restoring life's viability. Psychoanalytic practice is also interested primarily in phenomena of expenditure (deriving from inhibition, compulsion, and the like), despite its ideological and (in Freud's case, at least) in some ways atavistic attachment to finality. We see only a massive reinvestment of meaning in response to this common and recent disaffection with the production and promotion of meaning in the West. The supposed remedy is a primal regression to the religious (with or without "religion"): a return to the "sacred," to the question of evil, to God.

Faced with this, philosophy has, I think, been slow to react and has largely lacked the means to do so. Clearly, these developments have forced it to adopt a new program. The absence of ends is not something it needs to hide or compensate for. If it tries to do so, all it will do is just recycle obsolete ideologies. The task of philosophy today is, I believe, above all to reconsider its insistence on meaning, which has driven it to this point, and to ponder "existence" as a replacement for the quest for truth. To that end, it needs to draw on the cultural choices of other civilizations in order to challenge its own anthropological presuppositions more radically. It can use these other civilizations to reflect on itself. The goal is not to "expand our concepts" in the sense of subsuming a broader diversity, as philosophy has claimed to do since its globalization. It is, rather, to subject itself to a fundamental — and, for philosophy, unprecedented — derangement, comparable to the derangement of which, in our time, art alone has shown itself capable. The point would be to reveal the whole range of options and assumptions philosophers have unwittingly adopted to determine philosophy's quite distinctive fate. For hasn't art always been ahead of philosophy? (And is it not alone in the contemporary period in having attempted, through its practice, to uproot itself?) Art today demonstrates how a practice can explore diverse cultures in order to purge its atavisms and reinvent itself. Without giving in to facile exoticism, philosophy can take a more rigorous approach to revising its universal vocation. This can lead to a bolder (and more triumphal) strategy for reoccupying its traditional terrain, where the need for it is urgently felt — in morality and politics above all.

Notes

PREFACE

1. François Jullien, *Un sage est sans idée; ou, L'autre de la philosophie* (Paris: Seuil, 1998).

2. François Jullien, *Du "temps": Eléments d'une philosophie du vivre* (Paris: Grasset, 2001).

3. François Jullien, *L'ombre au tableau: Du mal ou du négatif* (Paris: Seuil, 2004).

4. François Jullien, *La grande image n'a pas de forme; ou, Du non-objet par la peinture* (Paris: Seuil, 2003).

5. Unless another edition is specified, I refer throughout to the following edition: Zhuangzi, *Jiao zheng Zhuangzi ji shi*, ed. Guo Qingfan (Taipei: Shi jie shu ju, 1962), 2 vols. (For a French translation, see *L'oeuvre complète de Tchouang-tseu*, trans. Liou Kia-hway [Liu Jiahuai] [Paris: Gallimard, 1969]. Partial English translations exist: *Chuang-tzu: The Seven Inner Chapters and Other Writings from the Book Chuang-tzu*, trans. A.C. Graham [London: Allen and Unwin, 1981]; *The Complete Works of Chuang Tzu*, trans. Burton Watson (New York: Columbia University Press, 1968); and *Chuang Tzu: Basic Writings*, trans. Burton Watson [New York: Columbia University Press, 1964]. I have translated the passages commented on in the text from the author's French, which frequently departs considerably from the published translated versions — TRANS.)

CHAPTER ONE: FEEDING THE BODY/FEEDING THE SOUL

1. Henri Crouzel, *Origène et la "connaissance mystique"* (Pairs: Desclée de Brouwer, 1961), pp. 166–79.

2. André Gide, *Les Nourritures terrestres* (Paris, 1897).

3. Yang Zhu; cf. Gaozi's position in the *Mencius*: Mengzi, *Mencius* 6a–b.

4. See Zhuangzi, *Jiao zheng Zhuangzi ji shi*, ed. Guo Qingfan (Taipei: Shi jie shu ju, 1962), ch. 19, p. 644.

5. Aristotle, *Nicomachean Ethics* 1.7.1097b32.

6. Zhuangzi, *Zhuangzi,* ch. 3, p. 115.

7. Henri Maspero, "Methods of 'Nourishing the Vital Principle' in the Ancient Taoist Religion," *Taoism and Chinese Religion*, trans. Frank A. Kierman Jr. (Amherst: University of Massachusetts Press, 1981), pp. 443–54.

8. Zhuangzi, *Zhuangzi*, ch. 1, p. 28; ch. 6, p. 252; ch. 12, p. 421.

9. *Ibid.*, ch. 6, p. 252.

10. *Ibid.*, ch. 11, p. 381.

11. *Ibid.*, ch. 20, p. 695.

12. See, for example, *ibid.*, ch. 2, p. 74, and ch. 5, p. 222.

13. *bid.*, ch. 6, p. 226.

14. *Ibid.*, ch. 12, p. 609.

15. Honoré de Balzac, *The Magic Skin*, trans. Ellen Marriage (New York: Charles Scribner's Sons, 1915), p. 269.

CHAPTER TWO: PRESERVING THE FREEDOM TO CHANGE

1. Zhuangzi, *Jiao zheng Zhuangzi ji shi*, ed. Guo Qingfan (Taipei: Shi jie shu ju, 1962), ch. 19, p. 630.

2. *Ibid.*, ch. 3, p. 115.

CHAPTER THREE: TO FEED ONE'S LIFE / TO FORCE ONE'S LIFE

1. Zhuangzi, *Jiao zheng Zhuangzi ji shi*, ed. Guo Qingfan (Taipei: Shi jie shu ju, 1962), ch. 6, p. 252; see p. 17 above.

2. *Ibid.*, ch. 19, p. 632; see p. 27 above.

3. Zhuangzi, *L'oeuvre complète de Tchouang-tseu*, trans. Liou Kia-hway [Liu

Jiahuai] (Paris: Gallimard, 1969), p. 70, and *Chuang-tzu: The Seven Inner Chapters and Other Writings from the Book Chuang-tzu*, trans. A.C. Graham (London: Allen and Unwin, 1981), p. 87.

4. See Zhuangzi, *Zhuangzi*, p. 255.

5. *Ibid.*, p. 254.

6. *Ibid.*, pp. 224 and 229.

7. See Mengzi, *Mencius* 7a26.

8. See Hanfeizi, *Han Fei Tzu* 20.

9. Laozi, *Laozi* 7.

10. *Ibid.*, 22.

11. *Ibid.*, 34.

12. *Ibid.*, 50.

13. *Ibid.*, 55.

14. John 12:25.

15. John 12:24.

16. Laozi, *Laozi* 40, 68, 66, 78.

17. *Ibid.*, 38.

18. *Ibid.*, 41 and 45.

19. Zhuangzi, *Zhuangzi*, ch. 5, p. 220.

20. *Ibid.*, p. 217.

CHAPTER FOUR: VACATIONS

1. Zhuangzi, *Jiao zheng Zhuangzi ji shi*, ed. Guo Qingfan (Taipei: Shi jie shu ju, 1962), ch. 6, p. 241.

2. See *ibid.*, ch. 15, p. 539.

3. *Ibid.*, ch. 6, p. 228.

4. *Ibid.*, ch. 19, p. 638.

5. *Ibid.*, ch. 6, p. 224.

6. *Ibid.*, ch. 15, p. 539.

7. *Ibid.*

8. *Ibid.*, ch. 19, p. 658.

9. Henri Matisse, "Lettre à André Rouveyre sur le dessin de l'arbre," *Ecrits*

et propos sur l'art, ed. Dominique Fourcade (Paris: Hermann, 1972), pp. 166–67.

10. Zhuangzi, *Zhuangzi*, ch. 2, p. 70.

11. *Ibid.*, ch. 19, p. 633.

12. *Ibid.*, p. 636.

13. *Ibid.*, ch. 20, p. 675.

14. *Ibid.*, p. 677.

15. *Ibid.*, ch. 19, p. 654.

CHAPTER FIVE: WITHOUT "SOUL"

1. Zhuangzi, *Jiao zheng Zhuangzi ji shi*, ed. Guo Qingfan (Taipei: Shi jie shu ju, 1962), ch. 2, p. 83.

2. Plato, *Phaedo* 64c–d.

3. Homer, *Odyssey* 11.220s.

4. Laozi, *Laozi* 12.

5. Plato, *Timaeus* 44d. R.B. Onians has found that the idea of the head as seat of the soul is common to the Celts and many Indo-European peoples: *The Origins of European Thought about the Body, the Mind, the Soul, the World, Time, and Fate* (Cambridge: Cambridge University Press, 1951), pp. 95–122.

6. Note, by the way, that recent translators of Freud coined the adjective "mental" to render the German seelisch, refusing to allow it to be subsumed any longer by the "psychic."

7. See, for example, Qu Yuan, "The Summons of the Soul [*Zhao hun*]," *Songs of the South*, ed. and trans. David Hawkes (Harmondsworth: Penguin, 1985), pp. 101–19, from the third century BCE.

8. Compare Zhuangzi, *Zhuangzi*, ch. 15, p. 539.

9. *Ibid.*, ch. 5, pp. 199, 212.

10. *Ibid.*, p. 632.

11. Zhuangzi, *L'oeuvre complète de Tchouang-tseu*, trans. Liou Kia-hway [Liu Jiahuai] (Paris: Gallimard, 1969), p. 150.

12. Zhuangzi, *Zhuangzi*, ch. 22, p. 741.

13. *Ibid.*, ch. 5, p. 544.

14. "To spiritualize and spiritualize more so as to attain quintessence," *ibid.*, ch. 12, p. 411.

15. Though some, including Marcus Aurelius (*Meditations* 2.2), tried to reduce man to a mere composite of "flesh," "breath," and an "internal guide" (*hēgemonikon*), the European subject nevertheless addresses his soul: "Oh, my soul! Will you ever be good, righteous, single, naked, and more visible than the body that envelops you?" (*ibid.*, 10.1).

16. Zhuangzi, *Zhuangzi*, ch. 5, p. 193.

17. *Ibid.*, p. 206.

Chapter Six: Do We Have a "Body"?

1. Excitement is represented in psychic life by the drive "*dessen Reiz im Seelenleben durch den Trieb repräsentiert ist*": Sigmund Freud, "Instincts and Their Vicissitudes," *Collected Papers*, trans. Joan Riviere (New York: Basic Books, 1959), pp. 60–83.

2. *Shen-ti* in classical Chinese can include the spirit's activity of knowing along with its other functions, in particular sensory perception. Thus it signifies the constitutive being of the person taken as a whole. For example, in the *Yueji*: "The indolent and depraved breath must not be introduced into the *shen-ti*, so that the various senses as well as the spirit's activity of knowing and all physical elements implement equity by adhering to rectitude" (*Liji*, ch. 2, para. 5). It thus commonly refers to the most comprehensive conception of health and full vitality.

3. Zhuangzi, *Jiao zheng Zhuangzi ji shi*, ed. Guo Qingfan (Taipei: Shi jie shu ju, 1962), p. 746.

4. *Ibid.*, ch. 4, p. 165.

5. See *ibid.*, ch. 20, p. 698, and ch. 12, p. 416.

6. *Ibid.*, ch. 22, p. 741.

7. *Ibid.*, ch. 18, p. 615. I translate as literally as I can here so as not to substantialize and therefore ontologize the Chinese sentence according to the mold of a foreign grammar.

8. See *ibid.*, ch. 12, p. 425.

9. See *ibid.*, ch. 18, p. 609.

10. *Ibid.*, ch. 12, p. 411.

11. "Our body can only be engendered by the Dao. Our life can only be manifested by virtue. He who preserves his health will live to an advanced age." Zhuangzi, *L'oeuvre complète de Tchouang-tseu*, trans. Liou Kia-hway [Liu Jiahuai] (Paris: Gallimard, 1969), p.101.

12. Mengzi, *Mencius* 6a14. Mencius, *The Works of Mencius*, ed. and trans. James Legge (New York: Dover, 1970), pp. 416–17.

13. *Ibid.*, 7a38.

14. Cf. Zhu Xi.

15. Mengzi, *Mencius* 7a21.

CHAPTER SEVEN: FEEDING YOUR BREATH-ENERGY

1. See, for example, Wang Chong, "Lun si," *Lunheng zhushi* (Beijing; Zhonghua shujo, 1979), vol. 3, p. 1186.

2. Zhuangzi, *Jiao zheng Zhuangzi ji shi*, ed. Guo Qingfan (Taipei: Shi jie shu ju, 1962), ch. 22, p. 733.

3. *Ibid.*, ch. 19, pp. 633–34.

4. *Ibid.*, p. 658; see above, p. 49.

5. Pablo Picasso, *Propos sur l'art*, ed. Marie-Laure Bernadac and Androula Michael (Paris: Gallimard, 1998), p. 123. In another interview, the question of longevity logically comes up again: "He [Picasso] could work three or four hours in a row without a superfluous gesture. I ask him if standing so long tired him. He shook his head. 'No. While I'm working, I leave my body at the door, as Muslims take off their shoes before entering a mosque. In this state, the body exists in a purely vegetal sense, and that is why we painters generally live so long'" (p. 117).

6. Zhuangzi, *Zhuangzi*, ch. 19, pp. 633–34.

7. *Ibid.*, p. 650.

8. Marcus Aurelius, *Meditations* 2.2.

9. Zhuangzi, *Zhuangzi*, ch. 6, p. 228.

10. *Ibid.*

11. See *ibid.*, ch. 15, p. 535.

12. On gymnastic and respiratory techniques of nourishment, see especially Chen Yaoting, Li Ziwei, and Liu Zhongyu, *Dao jia yang sheng shu* (Shanghai: Fudan da xue chubanshe, 1992), as well as two chapters in the important Japanese compilation by Yasuyori Tamba: *The Essentials of Medicine in Ancient China and Japan, Yasuyori Tamba's Ishimpo*, ed. and trans. Emil C.H. Hsia (Leiden: Brill, 1986), pt. 2, bks. 26 ("On Obtaining Longevity") and 27 ("Vital Nourishment").

13. Confucius, *The Analects* 16.7.

14. On the relationships among these different notions, see Xiao Tianshi, *Dao jia yang sheng xue gai yao* (Zhengzhou: Zhongzhou guji chubanshe, 1988), esp. p. 203.

15. Mengzi, *Mencius* 2a2.

CHAPTER EIGHT: PROCEDURES OF VITAL NOURISHMENT

1. Zhuangzi, *Jiao zheng Zhuangzi ji shi*, ed. Guo Qingfan (Taipei: Shi jie shu ju, 1962), ch. 3, p. 117.

2. Martin Heidegger, *Being and Time*, trans. John Macquarrie and Edward Robinson (New York: Harper, 1962), sec. 15.

3. Zhuangzi, *Zhuangzi*, ch. 3, p. 117.

4. Jean-François Billeter, *Leçons sur Tchouang-tseu* (Paris: Allia, 2002), p. 15ff.

5. Zhuangzi, *Zhuangzi,* ch. 7, p. 295, and ch. 12, p. 427.

6. I translated this as "when the knowledge of the senses ends" rather than as "my senses no longer came into play." This is closer to the text, for "when the knowledge of the senses ends," my refined apprehension, which is in the process of becoming spiritual, takes over.

7. Cf. Cheng Xuanying.

8. Plato, *Phaedrus* 265a–66c, 273e, 277b.

9. Zhuangzi, *Zhuangzi*, ch. 19, p. 639.

10. *Ibid.*, p. 641.

11. *Ibid.*, p. 656.

12. *Ibid.*, p. 662.

13. *Ibid.*, p. 660.

CHAPTER NINE: EXEMPT FROM HAPPINESS

1. Zhuangzi, *Jiao zheng Zhuangzi ji shi*, ed. Guo Qingfan (Taipei: Shi jie shu ju, 1962), ch. 15, p. 539.

2. Laozi, *Laozi* 18.

3. Zhuangzi, *Zhuangzi*, ch. 12, p. 416.

4. Aristotle, *Nicomachean Ethics* 1 and 10.

5. Sigmund Freud, *Civilization and Its Discontents*, trans. James Strachey (New York: Norton, 1961), p. 25.

6. As a final example of this philosophical stupidity, consider the opening words of Alice Germain's preface in André Comte-Sponville, Jean Delumeau, and Arlette Farge, *La plus belle histoire du bonheur* (Paris: Seuil, 2004): "Living is not enough; we also want to live happily. Existence has no meaning or zest unless it becomes a place and time of happiness. We expect happiness of life, so much so that we sometimes spend our lives waiting for it" (p. 9).

7. See especially Sigmund Freud, "Instincts and Their Vicissitudes," *Collected Papers*, trans. Joan Riviere (New York: Basic Books, 1959), pp. 63–65.

8. G.W. F. Hegel, *Phenomenology of Spirit*, trans. A.V. Miller (Oxford: Clarendon, 1977), p. 107.

9. The French translation given in Donald Holzman, *La vie et la pensée de Hi K'ang (223–262 ap. J.-C.)* (Leiden: Brill, 1957), p. 43, reads "Hi K'ang [Xi Kang] asked about his goal in life, but he never answered." But the Chinese text says something quite different: "He asked about his prepared plan [or blueprint]." *Tu* means map, drawing, or graphic.

10. In classical Chinese, *di* commonly means "target," as can be seen in the *Shijing* and the *Liji*. It also means "brilliant" (because it is highlighted, like a target) and "good example." The sense of "objective" is much rarer (see, for example, Hanfeizi, *Han Fei Tzu* 22: a sovereign would be wrong to listen to theories "without having their application as his objective," *bu yi gongyong wei di*). Indeed, it was the Legists who sketched out a rationalism of finality in reaction to the divinatory rationalism based on the deployment of correspondences. Hanfeizi, for instance, describes the discipline of archery not in ritualistic terms (involving certain prescribed gestures and positions) but in terms of a fixed goal

(to which the statesman must adjust his policy). The first use of the modern composite *mudi* to translate the Western "goal" is said to be in the *Xinerya*, written in 1903. I wish to thank Qi Chong for providing invaluable information on this subject.

11. Zhuangzi, *Zhuangzi*, ch. 19, p. 662.

12. *Ibid.*, ch. 6, p. 272.

13. Confucius, *Shijing, The Classic Anthology Defined*, trans. Ezra Pound (London: Faber, 1954).

14. Heraclitus, fr. 119, in Hermann Diels and Walther Kranz, *Die Fragmente der Vorsokratiker, griechisch und deutsch* (Berlin: Weidmann, 1934), vol. 1, p. 177.

15. Democritus, frs. 170–71, in Diels-Kranz, vol. 2, pp. 178–79.

16. Zhuangzi, *Zhuangzi*, ch. 15, p. 535.

17. *Ibid.*

18. Laozi, *Laozi* 38; see above, Chapter Three.

19. Zhuangzi, *Zhuangzi*, ch. 15, p. 539.

20. *Ibid.*, p. 544.

21. *Ibid.*, ch. 6, p. 226.

22. *Ibid.*, p. 243.

23. *Ibid.*

24. *Ibid.*, ch. 2, p. 70.

25. *Ibid.*, ch. 22, p. 745.

26. *Ibid.*, ch. 12, p. 440.

27. Paul Demiéville, "Le miroir spirituel," *Choix d'études bouddhiques* (Leiden: Brill, 1973), p. 131.

28. Zhuangzi, *Zhuangzi*, ch. 7, p. 307.

CHAPTER TEN: ON HYGIENE

1. Xi Kang, *Yang sheng lun*, ch. 53; translated into French in Donald Holzman, *La vie et la pensée de Hi K'ang (223–262 ap. J.-C.)* (Leiden: Brill, 1957) and into English in Robert G. Henricks, *Philosophy and Argumentation in Third-Century China: The Essays of Hsi K'ang* (Princeton, NJ: Princeton University Press, 1983).

2. Holzman, *La vie et la pensée*, p. 52.

3. Mengzi, *Mencius* 2a2.16.

4. Laozi, *Laozi* 64.

5. In China, the words for "to care for" and "to govern" are the same.[b] We also find a parallelism between the physical existence of the individual and the body of the state, as well as between the authority of the spirit and the power of the prince, the husbanding of vital energy and the accumulation of riches in the royal treasury, and so on.

6. See Jackie Pigeaud, *L'art et le vivant* (Paris: Gallimard, 1995), ch. 6; compare Per-Gunnar Ottosson, *Scholastic Medicine and Philosophy: A Study of Commentaries on Galen's Tegni, ca. 1300–1450* (Naples: Bibliopolis, 1984), ch. 3.

7. Francis Bacon, *De dignitate et augmentis scientiarum,* in *The Works of Francis Bacon*, eds. James Spedding and Robert Leslie Ellis (Boston: Brown and Taggart, 1860–64), vol. 1, p. 586.

8. *Ibid.*, p. 598.

9. Francis Bacon, *Historia Vitae et Mortis*, in *ibid.*, vol. 1, p. 159.

10. Bacon, *De dignitate et augmentis scientiarum* in *ibid.*, p. 598.

11. René Descartes, *Discourse on the Method, and Meditations on First Philosophy*, trans. Elizabeth S. Haldane and G.R.T. Ross, ed. David Weissman (New Haven: Yale University Press, 1996), ch. 6.

12. Immanuel Kant, *The Conflict of the Faculties: Der Streit der Fakultäten*, trans. Mary J Gregor (Lincoln: University of Nebraska Press, 1992), pt. 3.

13. Cf. Xiang Kang's refutation of his contemporary Xiang Xiu in *Nan Yang-sheng lun*, whom he challenged to a debate. Xi Kang's response to Xiang Xiu is in *Tan nan Yang-sheng lun*. Both can be found in *Philosophy and Argumentation in Third Century China*, trans. G. Henricks (Princeton, NJ: Princeton University Press, 1983), pp. 21–70.

CHAPTER ELEVEN: ANTI-STRESS

1. Zhuangzi, *Jiao zheng Zhuangzi ji shi*, ed. Guo Qingfan (Taipei: Shi jie shu ju, 1962), ch. 6, p. 229.

2. Galen, *On the Passions and Errors of the Soul*, trans. Paul W. Harkins, ed.

Walther Riese (Columbus: Ohio State University Press, 1963).

3. René Descartes to Princess Elizabeth, May or June 1645, in *Oeuvres et lettres*, ed. André Bridoux (Paris: Gallimard, 1953), p. 948.

4. *Ibid.*

5. Zhuangzi, *Zhuangzi*, ch. 4, p. 152.

6. *Ibid.*, ch. 7, p. 287.

7. *L'Oeuvre compléte de Tchouang-tseu*, trans. and preface Lion Kia-hway (Paris: Gallimard, 1973), p. 76; Chuang-tzu—*The Seven Inner Chapters and Other Writings from the Book Chuang-tzu*, trans. A.C. Graham (London: George Allen and Unwin, 1981), p. 94.

8. Zhuangzi, *Zhuangzi*, ch. 5, p. 212.

9. *Ibid.*, ch. 22, p. 737.

Chapter Twelve: Condemned to the Eternal Silence of Processes

1. Xi Kang, *Yang sheng lun*, in Robert G. Henricks, *Philosophy and Argumentation in Third-Century China: The Essays of Hsi K'ang* (Princeton, NJ: Princeton University Press, 1983), pp. 29–30.

2. Henricks, *Philosophy and Argumentation*, p. 30.

3. Laozi, *Laozi* 5.

4. Confucius, *The Analects* 4.10.

Glossary of Chinese Terms

CHAPTER ONE: FEEDING THE BODY/FEEDING THE SOUL
a. *Yang sheng* 養生
b. *Yang jing* 養精
c. *Xu rui* 畜銳
d. *Yang jing* 養靜
e. *Xue sheng* 學生
f. *Du* 督
g. *Chang sheng* 長生
h. *Shou* 守

CHAPTER TWO: PRESERVING THE FREEDOM TO CHANGE
a. *Jing* 精
b. *Jing er you jing* 精而又精
c. *Neng yi* 能移
d. *Yu bi geng sheng* 與彼更生

CHAPTER THREE: TO FEED ONE'S LIFE /
TO FORCE ONE'S LIFE
a. *Sheng* 生
b. *Zi sheng* 自生
c. *Yi sheng* 益生

173

d. *Qing* 情
e. *Ziran* 自然
f. *Tian yu, tian shi* 天鬻 ， 天食

CHAPTER FOUR: VACATIONS
a. *Cheng xin* 成心
b. *Ji* 機

CHAPTER FIVE: WITHOUT "SOUL"
a. *Hun* 魂
b. *Ling-fu, ling tai* 靈府, 靈臺
c. *Shen, jing-shen* 神 , 精神
d. *Di* 帝
e. *De* 德

CHAPTER SIX: DO WE HAVE A "BODY"?
a. *Xing, shen, ti* 形 , 身 , 體
b. *Shen, xin, qi* 身 , 心 , 氣
c. *Xing-hai, xing-qu, sizhi xing-ti, jiu qiao* 形骸 , 形軀 , 四枝開體 , 九竅
d. *Xing* 性 , *qing* 情
e. *Sheng-li* 生理
f. *Shen* 神
g. *Wei xing* 為形
h. *Wu yu wu* 物於物
i. *Ti* 體
j. *Guan* 官
k. *Jin xin* 盡心

CHAPTER SEVEN: FEEDING YOUR BREATH-ENERGY
a. *Qi* 氣
b. *Feng-jing* 風景

c. *Nei shi* 內視
d. *Shen-ren* 神人
e. *Haoran zhi qi* 浩然之氣

CHAPTER EIGHT: PROCEDURES OF VITAL NOURISHMENT

a. Cf. the classical expression: *Shen yu wu you* 神與物遊
b. *Ming* 命

CHAPTER NINE: EXEMPT FROM HAPPINESS

a. *Ze, er* 則, 而
b. *Zhong, tu di* 中, 圖 的
c. *Mudi, mubiao* 目的, 目標
d. *You* 遊
e. *Fu, lu, xiu* 福, 祿, 休
f *Yu zhu yong* 寓諸庸

CHAPTER TEN: ON HYGIENE

a. *Yang-sheng-fa* 養生法
b. *Zhi* 治
c. *Sheng-li* 生理
d. *Yong* 用; cf. *Zhouyi*, "Xici," A, 5, 藏諸用
e. *Sheng* 生
f. *Wu qiong* 無窮
g. *Bian-tong* 變通
h. *Jing* 精
i. *Wei* 徵

CHAPTER ELEVEN: ANTI-STRESS

a. *Xiaoran* 翛然
b. *You* 遊
c. *Yang zhong* 養中
d. *Tong* 通

Chapter Twelve: Condemned to the Eternal Silence of Processes

a. *Shen-qi* 神氣

b. *Li* 理

c. *Zi de* 自得

d. *Shen cun* 身存

Zone Books series design by Bruce Mau
Typesetting by Archetype
Printed and bound by Maple-Vail